# TIMEFRAME

## THE ILLUSTRATED HISTORY

### DAVID J. HOWE

DOCTOR WHO BOOKS

Sleeve painting by Alistair Pearson/Alistrations (1990) for the BBC Video *Doctor Who - An Unearthly Child*. Painting also used on Virgin Publishing's 1990 re-issue of *Doctor Who - An Unearthly Child* by Terrance Dicks (1981, W. H. Allen & Co. Ltd).

## BY THE SAME AUTHOR:

(with Mark Stammers and Stephen James Walker)
**Doctor Who The Sixties**
**Doctor Who The Seventies**
**Doctor Who The Handbook: The First Doctor**
**Doctor Who The Handbook: The Fourth Doctor**
**Doctor Who The Handbook: The Sixth Doctor**

(with David B. Wake)
**Doctor Who: Drabble Who**

# ACKNOWLEDGEMENTS

In preparing this book I must acknowledge a debt of gratitude to a number of people.

First to Mark Stammers who undertook all the design and layout of this book. Any impact it has is down to him.

Next, to the artists, all of whom kindly agreed that we could reproduce their work here. Thanks to Chris Achilleos, Peter Brooks, Ian Burgess, Tony Clark, Jeff Cummins, Bill Donohoe, John Geary, Colin Howard, Steve Kyte, Tony Masero, David McAllister, Alister Pearson and Andrew Skilleter. Especial thanks to Lesley Jarrett, wife of the late Alun Hood, for agreeing to his work being represented. She has requested that Alun's fee be donated to the Great Ormond Street Children's Hospital and if you would like to make a donation to this worthy cause, please send a cheque with your donation made payable to Great Ormond Street Ltd and send it to Great Ormond Street Children's Hospital Fund, 49 Great Ormond Street, London, WC1N 3HZ, England.

Thanks to *Doctor Who Magazine*, Graeme Wood and Stephen James Walker who allowed me to rummage through and pillage their collections. To Andrew Pixley for his eagle eye, and to those who responded to my cry for help: David Burke, Peter Chandler, Sean Coleman, Ian Johnson, Richard Payne, John Pettigrew, Alex Saville, Jeremy Spencer, K Wilkinson and Peter Wylde. Ruth Salisbury of the Creative Licensing Corporation, Roger Coombes for the loan of Andrew Skilleter's *Logopolis* artwork

Respect is due to Gary Russell, who has helped immeasurably with advice and information and who likes artwork as much as I do. Final thanks to Anne Gilmore who knows why this credit is here.

## PHOTOGRAPH AND ILLUSTRATION CREDITS

Thanks to the following people whose photographs have been used in this book: **AC** - Anthony Clark, **BN** - Barry Newbery, **DH** - David J. Howe, **GW** - Graeme Wood, **JML** - John McLay, **PA** - Paul Allen, **PR** - Paul Rogers, **RC** - Raymond P. Cusick, **RMD** - Ronald McDevitt, **RP** - Robin Pritchard, **SM** - Susan Moore. All other photographs are copyright BBC. Every attempt has been made to track down individual copyright holders and we apologise if anyone has been inadvertently missed.

First published in Great Britain in 1993 by
Doctor Who Books
An Imprint of Virgin Publishing Ltd
332 Ladbroke Grove
London W10 5AH

This edition first published in 1994

Cover and interior design by
Mark Stammers Design
London

Printed and bound by Printeksa (Spain)

ISBN 0 86369 861 1

# CONTENTS

Jacket painting by Chris Achilleos (1976) for the revised edition of *The Making of Doctor Who*
by Terrance Dicks and Malcolm Hulke (1976, Tandem Publishing Ltd, first published by Pan Books in 1972).

# DEDICATION

Dedicated to fans of the Doctor all over the world, and in particular: to Jeremy Bentham, whose enthusiasm fired my own; to Jan Vincent-Rudzki, Stephen Payne and Keith Barnfather, who fanned the flames; and to Mark Stammers and Stephen James Walker for keeping it fun.

Jacket painting by David McAllister (1980) for *Doctor Who and the Keys of Marinus* by Philip Hinchcliffe (1980, W. H. Allen & Co. Ltd)

# INTRODUCTION

**W**elcome to the illustrated history of *Doctor Who*.

November 1963 saw the start of a television phenomenon. *Doctor Who* mixed science fiction and historical drama in a wide variety of story-telling styles; it could send you scurrying behind the sofa in terror, it could make you laugh, and it was enjoyed as much by adults as children.

Twenty six years and thirteen days after the first episode, *An Unearthly Child*, was transmitted, the BBC aired the final episode of *Survival*, the last *Doctor Who* story. But this wasn't the end. The Doctor and his timeship, the TARDIS, had transcended the TV screen and rematerialised in comics and in novels, on film and on stage, in toyshops and on video. In the nineties, thirty years on, *Doctor Who* is as popular as it has ever been. The Doctor's adventures continue to be released on video and repeated extensively on both terrestrial and satellite television. All over the world conventions and other events celebrate one of the great cultural icons of the twentieth century.

As well as celebrating thirty years of the Doctor's travels, this book marks a remarkable publishing feat. In 1973 the Universal Tandem Book Publishing Company obtained the rights to three *Doctor Who* novels which had first been published in the sixties. They arranged for an up and coming artist called Chris Achilleos to paint startling new cover illustrations for the books which did so well that the publisher commissioned *Doctor Who*'s then script editor, Terrance Dicks, to novelise some more adventures. Twenty years on, the astonishing range of *Doctor Who* books is still going strong.

The emphasis in this book is on the visual aspects of the series and the novels. Inside you can meet both friends and foes, relive some of *Doctor Who*'s classic moments and recall the many events in *Doctor Who*'s history.

Fasten your safety belt as we plunge back in time to 23 November 1963.

**David J. Howe**
April 1993

# THE SIXTIES

The first mention of the fledgling BBC drama series *Doctor Who* was in the 14 November edition of *Radio Times*. The following week Kenneth Horne peered out from the cover of the BBC's listings magazine and on Saturday, 23 November, at 5:16:20, *Doctor Who* began.

No one at the BBC expected *Doctor Who* to become the success it did, but the introduction of the Daleks in December 1963 assured its survival. The Daleks were the first alien menace to appear on *Doctor Who*, and Terry Nation's story of a race of mutants living in robotic shells in a metal city on the edge of a petrified forest was to become a television classic.

Originally devised as a partly educational series, *Doctor Who* initially balanced its historical output with other science-fiction-based tales. However, as the series progressed, the emphasis shifted more firmly towards adventure and drama in outer space.

Almost coinciding with this shift was the groundbreaking decision to change the actor playing the Doctor. William

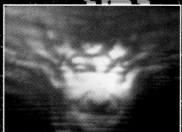

Hartnell had enchanted a generation of viewers with his portrayal of the Doctor as an intensely moral, intelligent and occasionally irascible grandfather figure, but he had been ill for some time, and the show's producers decided to replace him. The rationale was to be that the Doctor had a hitherto unsuspected ability which would become known as regeneration. The second Doctor was played by Patrick Troughton, and was markedly different from his predecessor. Younger and sprightlier, Troughton played the time traveller as a whimsical and unpredictable cosmic Charlie Chaplin. With compassion for all, and steely nerves in the face of evil, the Doctor battled on until he was finally captured and put on trial by his own people, the Time Lords.

The Doctor's trial formed a fitting climax to the black and white era of the programme. The Daleks had brought *Doctor Who* into the public eye, and the country had become gripped with Dalekmania. Over one hundred different toys, games, records and books were released to tie in with the programme, as well as two cinema films, starring Peter Cushing as the Doctor, and a London stage play. As well as the Daleks, silver Cybermen, Ice Warriors from Mars, robot Yeti, deadly Quarks, chirruping Zarbi, peaceful Sensorites and slimy crablike Macra, all invaded living rooms across the country.

*Doctor Who* had arrived.

# Season One

**D**octor Who bursts on our TV screens in flickering black and white, heralded by eerie throbbing music and un-earthly swirling patterns. We are introduced to the Doctor, his grand-daughter Susan, and her human teachers Ian and Barbara. The Doctor's space/time craft, the TARDIS, makes its debut in the shape of a battered London police telephone box and the Doctor and his companions are thrown back in time where they help a stone-age tribe re-discover the secret of fire. Attempting to return to their own time, they travel instead to the dead planet of Skaro where the hideously mutated Daleks lurk in a metal city while the beautiful

**A signed photograph of William Hartnell sent out to fans.**

## Dr. Who

SATURDAY'S serial begins when two teachers (**Jacqueline Hill** and **William Russell**) probe the mystery surrounding one of their pupils (**Carol Ann Ford**)—and meet the strange Dr. Who

**The Daleks in their metal city on Skaro (*The Daleks* December 1963) [RC].**

Thals live in the dead forests around it. The Daleks intend to wipe out the Thals and the time travellers become involved in the battle to prevent this. Upon returning to the TARDIS, they inadvert-ently plunge back towards the very creation of time before arriving on the Pamir Plateau in 1289 where they join Marco Polo on a journey to Peking. From there they travel to the planet Marinus where they are co-opted to hunt for

### 5.15
**DR. WHO**

An adventure in space and time
with
**WILLIAM HARTNELL**
*as* Dr. Who
**WILLIAM RUSSELL**
*as* Ian Chesterton
**JACQUELINE HILL**
*as* Barbara Wright
and
**CAROLE ANN FORD**
*as* Susan Foreman

**An Unearthly Child**

by ANTHONY COBURN
Title music by RON GRAINER
and the
BBC Radiophonic Workshop
Incidental music by
NORMAN KAY
Story editor, David Whitaker
Designer, Peter Brachacki
Associate producer,
Mervyn Pinfield
Producer, VERITY LAMBERT
Directed by WARIS HUSSEIN
*See page 7*

**Radio Times programme listing for the first episode of *Doctor Who* and a 'teaser' photograph.**

See page 7

## Magic Moments
### 100,000 BC (1963)

'No, grandfather,' screamed Susan. 'Mr Chesterton, stop him. He's start-ing the ship. We're going to take off!'

Instinctively, Ian leaped across the control room, and grappled with the Doctor. Once again he discov-ered that the old man was far stronger than he looked. With a mighty effort, Ian managed to drag the Doctor away from the console. But suddenly the old man twisted in his grasp, dashed to the console and pulled what was obviously some kind of master switch. The whole control room seemed to spin like a top. Ian and Barbara were both hurled from their feet, and everything went black ...

**From the novelisation by Terrance Dicks (1981)**

Jacket painting by Chris Achilleos (1973) for *Doctor Who and the Daleks* by David Whitaker (1973, Universal-Tandem Publishing Co. Ltd, originally published as *Doctor Who in an exciting adventure with the Daleks* by Frederick Muller Ltd in 1964).

Marco Polo (Marc Eden) falsely accuses the Doctor of hoarding water (*Marco Polo* February 1964).

the keys to a dormant thought-control machine. Barbara is mistaken for the reincarnation of an Aztec priest when they arrive in Mexico on Earth around 1430 and she unsuccessfully tries to stop the practice of human sacrifice. The TARDIS next arrives on a spaceship orbiting the Sense Sphere, home of the telepathic Sensorites. The Sensorites are dying out and the Doctor helps them discover the cause. Finally the Doctor and his friends become involved in intrigues during the French Revolution of 1794.

*Doctor Who* appears on the cover of *Radio Times* for the first time (February 1964).

The Doctor and his TARDIS (*Marco Polo*).

Susan (Carole Ann Ford) watches as Ian (William Russell) and the Doctor enter the TARDIS' fantastic control room (*100,000 BC* November 1963) [BN].

## Magic Moments
### The Daleks (1963)

The answer came through the front entrance slowly. A nightmare answer that had the blood draining away from my face and the skin stretching around my eyes. It was a round metal thing about three feet in height, like an upturned beaker with a domed top. It had dull metal flanges all round it and three different kinds of rods sticking out in front. It glided over the metal flooring and Susan retreated before it until she stood close to me. Now I knew what it was I'd been conscious of, and what Susan had seen behind me, because I became aware that we were surrounded by more of them, all gliding out of the doors of the entrance chamber and pointing their rods at us.

From the novelisation by David Whitaker (1964)

Barbara (Jacqueline Hill) and Susan are taken for a rendezvous with the guillotine (*The Reign of Terror* August 1964).

**Jacket painting by Nick Spender (1984) for** *Doctor Who - The Aztecs* **by John Lucarotti (1984, W. H. Allen & Co. Plc).**

# Season Two

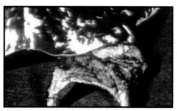

Top to Bottom, Left to Right: In the film *Doctor Who and the Daleks* (June 1965) we partially see what lives inside the Dalek casings. A Dalek on the sands of Aridius (*The Chase* May 1965) [RC]. Richard the Lionheart (Julian Glover) and friends (*The Crusade* March 1965). Press cutting from the *Daily Mail* 5 March 1965.

The TARDIS and its occupants are accidentally reduced to insect size when they arrive on Earth, and are threatened by a giant cat as well as by a scientist who has invented a dangerous insecticide. Moving on they arrive on in the twenty second century to find that Earth has been invaded by the Daleks, whom the Doctor defeats once more. The Doctor decides to leave Susan on Earth where she has fallen in love with a Dalek resistance fighter, and on Dido he meets a new companion, Vicki, whom he frees from the malign influence of her companion Bennett. The TARDIS arrives in 64 AD Rome where the travellers enjoy a rest before becoming involved in the affairs of some slave traders and the emperor Nero. Next, the TARDIS is drawn to the surface of the planet Vortis by the Animus, a parasitic web creature which is slowly taking over the planet. The

## BBC plans to bring the Daleks back to life

### By DOUGLAS MARLBOROUGH

THE Daleks are coming back. Those mechanical monsters from outer space who were killed off in B.B.C. TV's *Dr. Who* science fiction series last month are being brought back to life.

The reason? Viewers miss them. Children have written to the score to the B.B.C. saying they miss the Daleks dialect — they spoke in monosyllables.

Producer Verity Lambert said last night: "We didn't intend to bring the Daleks back: but we have changed our minds because of all these requests."

Two Daleks were sent to Dr. Barnardo's Homes — but the B.B.C. kept two others.

## NOW THE DALEKS MOVE IN FOR CINEMA INVASION

### By Daily Mail Reporter

THE Daleks, the metal monsters from B.B.C. TV's *Dr. Who* series, are invading the cinema.

A screen version of the programme is to be made at Shepperton Studios with Peter Cushing, Roy Castle and Jennie Linden.

The film, in colour, will be called *Dr. Who and The Daleks.* An all-metal Dalek city has been created at the studios.

Co-producer Milton Subotsky said yesterday: "We have taken the first seven episodes of the TV serial and have re-written them into a screen play."

**Left to Right: Press cutting from the *Daily Mail* 13 March 1965. A poster advertising the first Dalek film. The *Radio Times* heralds the return of the Daleks (November 1964).**

# Magic Moments

### *Planet of Giants* (1964)

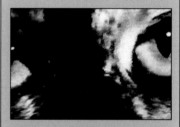

The cat was a terrifying sight, like a tiger as big as an elephant, thought Susan. The glowing green eyes seemed to have an almost hypnotic effect, and she felt a strange urge to run not away from but towards the cat.

'Don't move, any of you,' said Ian in a low voice.

**From the novelisation by Terrance Dicks (1990)**

Jacket painting by Anthony Clark (1987) for *Doctor Who - The Rescue* by Ian Marter (1987, W. H. Allen & Co. Plc).

Jacket painting by Tony Masero (1987) for *Doctor Who - The Romans* by Donald Cotton (1987, W. H. Allen & Co. Plc).

Doctor helps the peaceful Menoptra to rid themselves of the Animus. Back on Earth, this time in twelfth century Palestine, the Doctor becomes caught up in King Richard's Holy Crusade. Next, the time travellers arrive in a museum on the planet Xeros, in which they are themselves exhibited. They must work out how to change time and prevent this from happening. The Daleks are hot on the Doctor's trail and he leads them off on a chase through time and space. The Daleks are ultimately defeated by the Mechanoids and Ian and Barbara use their time machine to return to Earth. Steven, previously a prisoner of the Mechanoids, stows away on the TARDIS. They arrive in northeast England in 1066 to discover that another time traveller is trying to arrange for Harold to win the Battle of Hastings. The Doctor outwits the meddler and history is unchanged.

'Mum! It works!—Come and ask Dad!'

As Christmas approaches the Daleks invade toyshops: cartoon from the *Daily Mail* 19 December 1965. *Doctor Who* again features on the *Radio Times'* front cover (February 1965). The Daleks' first television adventure is released as a paperback novel (October 1965). The Doctor (Peter Cushing) confronts the Daleks (*Doctor Who and the Daleks* film). The first *Doctor Who* annual is released (September 1965).

## Magic Moments

### *The Dalek Invasion of Earth* (1964)

Quietly David said, 'He knew, Susan. He knew you would never leave him. That's why he left you.'

As David took Susan in his arms the TARDIS key slipped from her fingers, and lay unregarded on the ground. Susan made no attempt to pick it up because she knew she wouldn't be needing it again.

From the novelisation by Terrance Dicks (1977)

**Jacket painting by Chris Achilleos (1973) for *Doctor Who and the Zarbi* by Bill Strutton (1973, Universal-Tandem Publishing Co. Ltd, first published by Frederick Muller Ltd in 1965).**

# Season Three

On a doomed planet the Doctor encounters the evil but beautiful Drahvins and the good but ugly Rills, whom he helps to escape before the planet is destroyed. The TARDIS passes by the planet Kembel where the Daleks are plotting an invasion of the Solar System and arrives on Earth during the siege of Troy. The Doctor suggests the Greeks use a giant wooden horse to attack the city. Vicki stays in Troy as she has

The Trojan Horse (built for *The Myth Makers* October 1965) [DH].

fallen in love with Troilus, and a Trojan slave girl, Katarina, joins the TARDIS crew. The TARDIS materialises on Kembel where the Doctor struggles to prevent the Daleks from activating their Time Destructor and conquering the Solar System. During the course of the adventure Katarina is killed. The TARDIS arrives in Paris before the Saint Bartholomew's Day massacre in 1572 and the Doctor becomes involved in a Catholic plot to murder the Protestant Admiral de Coligny. During a brief stop on Wimbledon Common in the 1960s a young girl

The Doctor, Dodo (Jackie Lane) and Steven (Peter Purves) (*The Celestial Toymaker* April 1966).

Steven confronts the Toymaker (Michael Gough) (*The Celestial Toymaker*).

## Magic Moments

*The Daleks' Master Plan (1965)*

She suddenly knew what she must do. All her fear fell from her as she made her decision. Cassandra had been correct when she had prophesied her journeys. Now she would be correct about her fate. Katarina remembered how worried Bret had been about the airlock door being open when they had taken off from Kembal, and she had observed the Doctor operating the magic controls when they were on Desperus.

Before Kirksen could move closer, she jumped to her feet and brought her hand down hard on the outer door control.

Kirksen had time only to start a scream of sheer terror. The airlock door hissed open into the star-speckled darkness. The air shot both of them from the small chamber, sending them tumbling into infinity...

From the novelisation by John Peel (1989)

Jacket painting by Alistair Pearson/Allstrations (1989) for *Doctor Who - The Daleks' Masterplan: Part II - The Mutation of Time* by John Peel (1989, W. H. Allen & Co. Plc).

named Dodo enters the TARDIS and is whisked away to a space ark in the far future, where the cold virus she carries weakens the humans and allows the Monoid slaves to take control. The Doctor negotiates a peace between the two sides. The TARDIS is taken out of time by the Celestial Toymaker, an immortal mandarin-like character who forces the Doctor, Steven and Dodo to play games to win their freedom. The Doctor outwits the Toymaker and they escape. The Doctor develops toothache and they

arrive on Earth in the American West's town of Tombstone in 1881 to visit a dentist who is none other than Doc Holliday. The next stop is an alien planet where the civilised and intelligent Elders have been stealing life-force power from the local savages. Some of the Doctor's energy is taken, and

with it the leader of the Elders receives some of the Doctor's morality. Steven stays with them to help unite the sides. Arriving on Earth in 1966 the Doctor battles a computer called WOTAN which, from its base in the Post Office Tower in London, is trying to take over the world using robotic war machines. Dodo comes under the hypnotic influence of WOTAN and leaves to recover in the country; the Doctor is joined by two new companions, Ben and Polly.

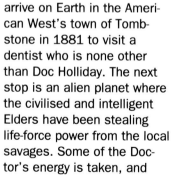

Clockwise from Top: A poster advertising the second Dalek film (June 1966). The second *Doctor Who* annual (September 1966). The Daleks appear on the London stage in David Whitaker's *The Curse of the Daleks* (December 1965). The Doctor wishes viewers a Merry Christmas in an episode transmitted on Christmas Day (*The Daleks' Master Plan*). Kert Gantry (Brian Cant) is exterminated (*The Daleks' Master Plan* November 1965). Ben Jackson (Michael Craze) joins the TARDIS crew (June 1966). The TARDIS arrives in the American Western town of Tombstone (*The Gunfighters* April 1966) [BN].

Jacket painting by Graham Potts (1986) for *Doctor Who - The Celestial Toymaker* by Gerry Davis and Alison Bingeman (1986, W. H. Allen & Co. Plc).

# Season Four

The TARDIS arrives in seventeenth century Cornwall and the Doctor, Ben and Polly become involved in smuggling. Jumping ahead in time, they arrive at an Antarctic space tracking station in 1986, just before it is invaded by the Cybermen. Ben and Polly help the humans on the base to repel the aliens, but the Doctor collapses from exhaustion and regenerates.

Culloden. They rescue a young piper, Jamie, and he joins them on their travels. They then visit the lost city of Atlantis where a crazed scientist is planning to drain the Earth's seas away and destroy the planet. Arriving on the moon in 2070, the Doctor helps when the Cyberman attack a lunar weather control station. On an Earth colony planet run like a holiday camp, the Doctor uncovers

and destroys a nest of crablike Macra which are controlling the humans from behind the scenes. The TARDIS arrives back at Gatwick Airport in England in 1966, where a race of faceless aliens are using an airline company as a cover for an operation taking the images of kidnapped humans as their own. The Doctor helps the aliens find another solution to their problem and

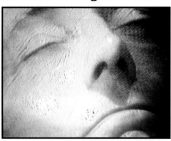

**The Doctor regenerates for the first time (*The Tenth Planet* October 1966).**

The TARDIS arrives on the planet Vulcan where an Earth colony is faced with extermination when a scientist reactivates a dormant Dalek; the Doctor cuts off the power and saves the colony. Back on Earth in 1746, the time travellers arrive in Scotland just after the battle of

**Above: The second Doctor with his recorder and diary (*The Power of the Daleks* November 1966). Left: The *Radio Times* heralds the new Doctor's battle with the Daleks (November 1966).**

## Magic Moments
### *The Tenth Planet* (1966)

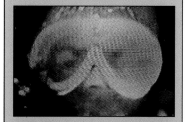

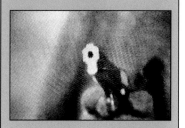

The Sergeant gazed, horror-struck, as they came nearer and nearer. He made out their chests — which resembled concertina-like packs. For heads, they had helmets with side handles, a mounted light, circles for eyes and a slit for a mouth. Seen at closer quarters they were much more like robots than human beings!

Jerking up his machine gun, he aimed and pulled the trigger. The mouth of the gun spurted fire and a stream of bullets sprayed across the marching figures. To his horror the bullets seemed to have no effect whatsoever! Not for one moment did they stop their steady march towards the two frightened men.

From the novelisation by Gerry Davis (1976)

Jacket painting by Alistair Pearson/Alistrations (1993) for *Doctor Who - The Power of the Daleks* by John Peel (1993, Virgin Publishing Ltd).

Jacket painting by Alistair Pearson/Alistrations (1993) for *Doctor Who - The Evil of the Daleks* by John Peel (1993, Virgin Publishing Ltd).

Ben and Polly decide to stay on Earth. While the Doctor is busy at the airport, the TARDIS is stolen on the orders of antiques dealer Edward Waterfield, setting in motion a complex plot to lure the Doctor to Skaro where the Daleks want to use the TARDIS to spread their evil throughout time and space. The Doctor instigates a Dalek civil war which results in their final end. Waterfield is killed in the fighting and his daughter Victoria travels on with the Doctor and Jamie.

Top Left: The Doctor sees the face of his previous incarnation in a hand-mirror (*The Power of the Daleks*). Top Right: The third *Doctor Who* annual (September 1967). Left: One of the slimy crab-like Macra (*The Macra Terror* March 1967). Below: The Dalek Emperor in his city on Skaro (*The Evil of the Daleks* May 1967).

## Magic Moments
*The Power of the Daleks* (1966)

The Dalek that had set the mechanism into motion now moved towards the seething pool. It paused beside it to slip its sucker-pad on to what looked like a large, metal fishing net. Then it glided alongside the liquid before lowering the net out of sight into the steaming waters. After a moment, the net was raised.

Lesterson saw what it contained and wanted to be sick.

From the novelisation by John Peel (1993)

Cover painting by Mick Anglo for *TV Tornado*, 1968.

Jacket painting by Bill Donohoe (1981) for W. H. Allen's re-issue of *Doctor Who and the Cybermen* by Gerry Davis (1975, Universal-Tandem Publishing Co. Ltd).

# Season Five

The Doctor, Jamie and Victoria arrive on the planet Telos where archæologists are excavating the frozen tombs of the Cybermen. The Cybermen are revived by a power-hungry logician but before they can take control the Doctor refreezes them. The Doctor visits Tibet in the 1930s and discovers that an alien intelligence is trying to establish a foothold on Earth by using the body of the High Lama and robot Yeti. The Doctor forces the intelligence back onto the astral plane. During Earth's third Ice Age, a frozen alien is discovered buried in a glacier. The Doctor prevents the revived Martian Ice Warrior Varga from freeing his ship and attempting to take over the world. In a near-future Australia the Doctor discovers that a dictator named Salamander – the Doctor's double

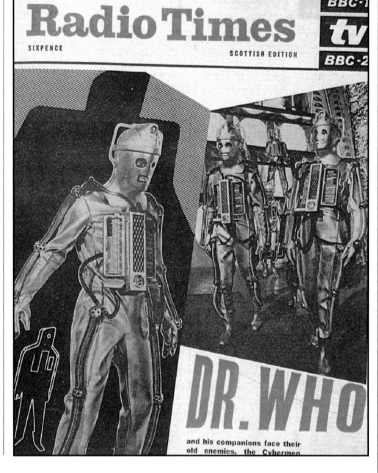

Top: *Radio Times* celebrates the return of the Cybermen (September 1967). Left: A Yeti (*The Abominable Snowmen* September 1967). Above: The deadly Cybermats (*The Tomb of the Cybermen* September 1967).

## Magic Moments
### The Tomb of the Cybermen (1967)

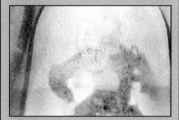

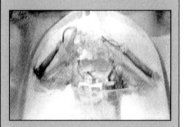

Another blow from his fist and the membrane was in shreds like a split drum. The Cyberman stiffly rose up and with his arms held out like a swimmer before him, pushed his way out of the cell and stood upright in front of the honeycomb.

The terrible blank stare of the Cyberman swept over the group of humans, to Klieg at the control desk and then back to the honeycomb as he turned to face the other emerging Cybermen. One by one the huge silver giants broke out of their centuries-old cells and climbed down to stand beside their companion.

From the novelisation by Gerry Davis (1978)

Final jacket painting by Bill Donohoe (1981) for *Doctor Who and the Enemy of the World* by Ian Marter. (1981, W. H. Allen & Co. Ltd).

– is creating volcanoes and earthquakes in an attempt to bring Earth to its knees. The Doctor manages to discredit him through impersonation. The TARDIS next arrives in the London underground system in the seventies and the travellers discover that the Great Intelligence has again invaded with its Yeti robots. Again, the Doctor repulses the Intelligence. Arriving near a North Sea gas

refinery, the Doctor helps repel an attack by a parasitic intelligent seaweed. Victoria decides to remain on Earth. The Doctor and Jamie travel on to a twenty-first century space wheel where they help avert another planned invasion of the Earth by the Cybermen. One of the wheel's crew, Zoe, stows away on the TARDIS.

**Above: An Ice Warrior stands by a sonic cannon (*The Ice Warriors* November 1967). Right, Top to Bottom: The *Radio Times* runs a full-colour feature on *Doctor Who* (January 1968). The fourth *Doctor Who* annual (September 1968). Zoe Herriot (Wendy Padbury) stows away on the TARDIS (*The Wheel In Space* April 1968). To accompany the picture cards given away with Sky Ray ice lollies, Wall's produced an attractive album (1967).**

EIGHTPENCE—NORTHERN IRELAND EDITION

JANUARY 20–2

# Radio Times

BBC **tv**

## THE MONSTROUS WORLD OF DOCTOR WHO

see centre pages

THE **DR WHO** ANNUAL

Wall's

Dr Who's Space Adventure Book

A SKY RAY publication by arrangement with BBC **tv**

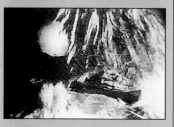

Jacket painting by Ian Burgess (1988) for *Doctor Who and the Wheel in Space* by Terrance Dicks (1988, W. H. Allen & Co. Plc).

Jacket painting by Chris Achilleos (1976) for Doctor Who and the Web of Fear by Terrance Dicks (1976, Wyndham Publications Ltd and Allan Wingate (Publishers) Ltd).

# Season Six

The Doctor, Jamie and Zoe find that the peaceful planet of Dulkis has been invaded by alien Dominators and their deadly robot Quarks. The Dominators want to turn the planet into a power source for their fleet but the Doctor stops them. However, the Dominators cause an island volcano to erupt and to escape, the TARDIS takes the time travellers to a land of fiction. The crew are hunted by clockwork soldiers, meet the Medusa and the Minotaur and are finally fictionalised by the land's Master Brain computer. They escape only to end up on Earth in the mid-seventies during another Cyberman invasion – this time through the London sewers. The Doctor, aided by UNIT, repels the Cybermen and heads off to the planet of the Gonds, who are slaves to the Dynatrope, a machine containing the crystalline

**Top: The Doctor is engulfed in alien foam (*The Seeds of Death* January 1969) [PA]. Bottom: The Toy Soldiers in the Land of Fiction (*The Mind Robber* September 1968).**

## DR WHO AND JAMIE TO QUIT BBC SHOW

THE BBC will lose its Dr Who, actor Patrick Troughton, and his companion Jamie, played by Frazer Hines, when the TV series reaches its summer break in June.

Troughton, who has played the role since he took over from William Hartnell, the original time-and-Space doctor, told the BBC that he wanted to leave in March.

But Producer Peter Bryant said last night: "He has agreed to stay on until June. I will then look for a replacement."

He added: "It is a blow to the series because Patrick has proved an excellent Dr. Who."

**Right: Press cutting from the *Daily Mirror* 7 January 1969.**

**Jacket painting by Andrew Skilleter (1985) for *Doctor Who - The Krotons* by Terrance Dicks (1985, W. H. Allen & Co. Plc).**

## Magic Moments

*The War Games (1969)*

Krotons. The Doctor destroys the Dynatrope with acid to free the Gonds. The TARDIS arrives in a twenty-first century space museum on Earth at the same time as the Ice Warriors invade the moon. The Doctor helps to destroy the Warriors and sends their invasion fleet into the Sun. Next, the travellers arrive on a space beacon and become involved in an intergalactic mineral piracy operation before returning to what seems to be Earth in the middle of the First World War. They have actually

arrived during a series of war games played by aliens to create an invincible human army. To return the kidnapped humans to their rightful places in time, the Doctor contacts his own people, the Time Lords, for help. They do, but they also place the Doctor on trial for interfering in the affairs of other planets. His sentence is to be exiled to Earth and for his appearance to be changed.

## TV SPACE SERIES GETS SHAKE-UP

# End of time for Dr Who

**COMEDIAN JON PERTWEE**
*He will star in colour.*

By BRIAN DEAN

BBC TV's perennial Dr Who comes to the end of his time-space travels tonight and is brought firmly down to earth after a once-and-for-all confrontation with the dreaded Daleks.

The serial is being given a completely new look—and a new Dr Who.

Comedian Jon Pertwee, star of the hit radio show *The Navy Lark*, will take over from 48-year-old former Shakespearean actor Patrick Troughton as Dr Who when the BBC1 Saturday evening serial returns in colour next January.

Mr Troughton will make his last appearance as the absent-minded doctor tonight when the current series ends.

He has told the BBC that after nearly three years as Dr Who he wants a change.

### Popular

It will also be the last appearance for Dr Who's companions Wendy Padbury, the 21-year-old pocket-sized actress who plays Zoe, and 23-year-old Frazer Hines, who plays Jamie.

Like Mr Troughton they have told the corporation that they want to leave the serial to go on to new acting jobs.

Their decision put the BBC spot. should the serial

**PATRICK TROUGHTON**
*Leaving series*

be scrapped or recast ? With eight million regular viewers, the BBC decided that the programme was too popular to lose and should be given a new lease of life in colour.

But the BBC has also decided to give the serial a completely new look.

Mr Pertwee, 50, said yesterday : 'It will be set on earth in the 1980s. I won't be wearing the Victorian clothes that the other Dr Who's have used. I will be in a modern day suit.'

The new Dr Who will have two companions — Nicholas Courtney, who will play the head of a special army unit and a scientist called Liz, who is still to be cast.

In tonight's episode Dr

**WILLIAM HARTNELL**
*The original Dr*

Who, who will come up against his own people, the Time Lords, and will meet again all the monsters that he has faced in his Tardis travels —Cybermen, Quarks, Yetis, Ice Warriors, and the Daleks.

### Younger

When Mr Troughton took over from William Hartnell, the original Dr Who, viewers saw the 900-year-old doctor going through a metamorphosis and appearing a few centuries younger.

At the end of tonight's episode Mr Troughton will be shown going through a similar change. And when the programme retuns it will be Mr Pertwee who appears as the doctor.

**Top Left: The Doctor regenerates for the second time (*The War Games* April 1969). Top Centre: The fifth *Doctor Who* annual (September 1969). Top Right: An Ice Warrior (*The Seeds of Death*) [PA]. Above Left: David and Alan Howe in an Edwin Hall Dalek kiddie ride (August 1968) [DH]. Above: Press cutting circa June 1969.**

The TARDIS stood exactly where the Doctor had left it. The sight of it urged him on. Soon all three were racing across flat open land and the Doctor was already fishing in his pockets for the key.

Zoe, running ahead, was the first to hit the force field. All at once she was struggling against something unseen, like a swimmer in thick treacle.

'Doctor,' she called back, 'what's happening?'

'We must concentrate,' the Doctor gasped. 'Help me with the key.'

From the novelisation by Malcolm Hulke (1979)

Jacket painting by Tony Masero (1986) for *Doctor Who - The Seeds of Death* by Terrance Dicks (1986, W. H. Allen & Co. Plc).

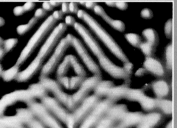

# THE SEVENTIES

**D**octor Who started the seventies with Jon Pertwee posing dramatically on the cover of the Radio Times, heralding the start of a new season in colour for the first time.

With a shift in emphasis from the nomadic Doctor of the sixties to the exiled and Earth-based Doctor of the early seventies, Doctor Who underwent some drastic realignment. Instead of the TARDIS, the Doctor's base of operations became a laboratory in UNIT HQ. UNIT – United Nations Intelligence Taskforce – had been introduced the previous season as an army-based group which dealt with unusual situations and problems both on Earth and beyond, and formed an ideal springboard for the Doctor's adventures.

The Doctor's companions – Liz Shaw, Jo Grant and then Sarah Jane Smith – were supplemented by a regular band of

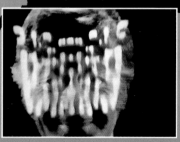

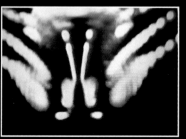

UNIT personnel – Brigadier Lethbridge-Stewart, Sergeant Benton and Captain Mike Yates – and together with the introduction of the Doctor's nemesis, the Master, formed a regular *Doctor Who* 'family'. After five years, Pertwee moved on and a little-known actor called Tom Baker was chosen to replace him.

Baker made the character of the Doctor his own. His trademark scarf and hat, together with his shock of curly brown hair and bulging eyes became synonymous with the time traveller, and Baker's wit and presence gave him the status of a cult hero. *Doctor Who* dabbled in horror, comedy and drama and for seven years Baker enthralled viewers across the world.

As the decade began on a high, so it ended on a low, with industrial action at the BBC forcing one *Doctor Who* adventure (*The Horns of Nimon*) to be hastily rewritten and restaged in studio and another (*Shada*) to be cancelled partway through recording. In the final season of the decade, *Doctor Who* turned to comedy and whimsy when Tom Baker's larger-than-life persona came to overshadow the programme. *Doctor Who* was moving into the eighties, and changes were afoot.

 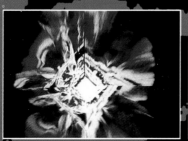  

# Season Seven

The Doctor's arrival on late twentieth century Earth to begin his exile coincides with a fall of alien meteorites containing the Nestene consciousness, a disembodied intelligence which is able to inhabit and animate anything made of plastic. The newly regenerated Doctor, together with a UNIT scientist, Liz Shaw, battle deadly plastic Autons to save the Earth. Not all threats come from space, as the Doctor discovers when a nest of hibernating intelligent reptiles under Wenley Moor is disturbed. The reptiles want to reclaim their planet and

**Above: The Brigadier (Nicholas Courtney).**

RADIO TIMES 1 JANUARY 1970

Midlands and E. Anglia Edition

BBC Radio Stoke-on-Trent Full details on page 66

John Williams Lunchtime Recital Radio 3: Monday

War & Peace Part 2 Radio 4: Tuesday

*RadioTimes*

Programmes for 3-9 January: Ninepence

New Shows for the New Year BBC1 & BBC2

Julie Driscoll in a play BBC1: Wednesday

A Question of Sport BBC1: Monday

Who?
Jon Pertwee,
that's Dr. Who
Saturday BBC1 Colour

**5.15** *Colour : New series*
**Dr Who**
starring **Jon Pertwee**
with **Caroline John**
and **Nicholas Courtney**
*Spearhead from Space*
by ROBERT HOLMES

**Part 1**
A swarm of 'meteorites' lands – and so does the *Tardis*. From it emerges a new Doctor – or is it an impostor? The new arrival is immediately an object of suspicion and a target for attack.

UNIT technician..........ELLIS JONES
UNIT Officer...............TESSA SHAW
Seeley.....................NEIL WILSON
Dr Who.................JON PERTWEE
Liz Shaw.............CAROLINE JOHN
Brigadier Lethbridge Stewart
　　　　　　　　NICHOLAS COURTNEY
Captain Munro........JOHN BRESLIN
Dr Henderson..........ANTONY WEBB
Nurse.................HELEN DORWARD
Mullins...............TALFRYN THOMAS
Corporal Forbes........GEORGE LEE
UNIT Soldier...............IAIN SMITH
Wagstaffe..........ALLAN MITCHELL
Second reporter..PRENTIS HANCOCK
Channing ..............HUGH BURDEN

Title music by RON GRAINER and the
BBC Radiophonic Workshop
Incidental music by DUDLEY SIMPSON
Script editor TERRANCE DICKS
Designer PAUL ALLEN
Producer DERRICK SHERWIN
Directed by DEREK MARTINUS †

**Top: Jon Pertwee on the cover of the *Radio Times* (January 1970). Far Left: A Silurian (*Doctor Who and the Silurians* January 1970). Left: *Radio Times* programme listing for the first episode of *Spearhead from Space* (January 1970). Above: A deadly plastic Auton (*Spearhead from Space*).**

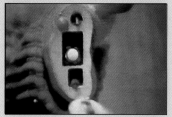

Jacket painting by Alistair
Pearson/Alistrations
(1992) for Virgin
Publishing's re-issue of
*Doctor Who - The Silurians*
by Malcolm Hulke (1974,
Universal-Tandem
Publishing Co. Ltd and
Allan Wingate (Publishers)
Ltd, originally published as
*Doctor Who and the Cave-
Monsters*).

the Doctor is on the verge of negotiating a peace when UNIT bomb their underground base, killing the leader and trapping the rest of the reptiles underground. Alien ambassadors visit the Earth, but are kidnapped, threatening a potential interplanetary war. The Doctor manages to pacify the aliens and bring the kidnappers to justice. Another menace comes from the very bowels of the Earth when a drilling project brings to the surface a noxious green slime which converts those who touch it into primordial creatures. The Doctor accidentally travels to a parallel Earth where the drilling splits the planet in two. Can he prevent the same from happening in his normal time stream?

**Top Right: Alien ambassadors visit the Earth (*The Ambassadors of Death* March 1970). Right: The sixth *Doctor Who* annual (September 1970). Far Right: A signed photograph of Jon Pertwee sent out to fans of the series.**

Jon Pertwee
Dr. WHO BBC TV

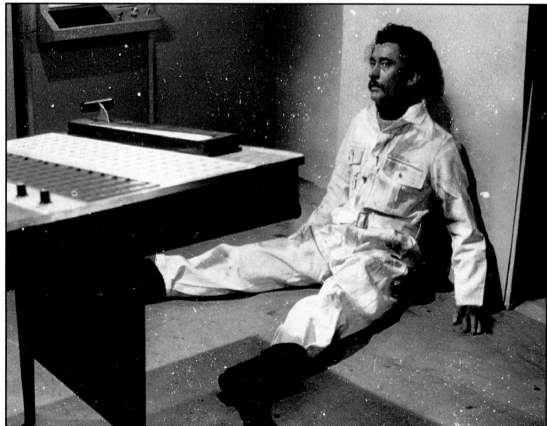

## Magic Moments

*The Ambassadors of Death* (1970)

Suddenly the door was flung open, obscuring the alien and the safe behind it. The Doctor paused for a moment, staring appalled at Quinlan's slumped body, then hurried forwards to the desk to examine it.

Satisfied that Quinlan was dead, the Doctor straightened up. The tall figure of the alien astronaut was stalking towards him, a gauntleted hand out-stretched ...

From the novelisation by Terrance Dicks (1987)

**Left: Harry Slocum (Walter Randall), turned into a Primord through contact with a noxious green slime, is killed (*Inferno* May 1970).**

**Jacket painting by Alistair Pearson/Alistrations (1991) for Virgin Publishing's re-issue of *Doctor Who - The Ambassadors of Death* by Terrance Dicks (1987, W. H. Allen & Co. Plc).**

# Season Eight

The Master, another renegade Time Lord, arrives on Earth with the intention of reopening an invasion channel for the Nestene consciousness. The Doctor, now with a new assistant, Jo Grant, is warned by the Time Lords and wins through. The Master does not give up easily and develops a plan to hijack a missile and use it to hold the Earth to ransom by threatening a vital peace conference. He also uses an alien mind-parasite to store evil from convicted prisoners and then projects this evil back onto those who stand in his way. The Doctor faces his greatest fears to defeat the Master. Leaving Earth, the Master is captured by Axos, another alien parasite, which lives off the energy of planets. The Master brings Axos to Earth in

Above Left: The Master (Roger Delgado) (*Terror of the Autons* January 1971). Above: The Axons reveal their true form (*The Claws of Axos* March 1971). Left: The emblem of the United Nations Intelligence Taskforce - UNIT. Below: An article from *Saturday Titbits* magazine on the making of *Doctor Who* (1971).

## Magic Moments

### The Mind of Evil (1971)

Monster after monster, terror after terror from the Doctor's past loomed up to attack him.

The Doctor could have dealt with any one of them, after all he'd met and defeated them all before ... But the steady, unremitting parade of horrors, combined with the atmosphere of pure fear generated by the Machine was eventually too much even for the Doctor ...

Suddenly panic overtook him. For a moment he writhed in vain against the bondage of the steel handcuffs – then his body gave a convulsive jerk and his head fell back.

From the novelisation by Terrance Dicks (1985)

---

Now that Daleks pass unnoticed a more terrifying creature has come stalking stealthily into our children's hours

SATURDAY TITBITS Page 25

The latest winged horror to walk into Dr. Who's world. And by the looks on the faces of Jon Pertwee and Katy Manning it isn't very welcome

# WHY MY MONSTERS ARE MARVELLOUS

## Dr. WHO TALKING TO ROGER WOODCOCK

Danger and fear lurk round every corner in the gory, violent world of Dr. Who. But monsters and murder may be setting youngsters up for frightening nights

... and choke people to death. Dolls strangling, and daffodils that are ... in the sick world of Teatime ... which policemen turn out to be ... their masks have been removed. ... Saturday millions of parents are ... to let their children watch ... serial that makes Dracula look

... took And ke. ... oved ... and things

... corner ... by the ... ques-Has the

... had ... said ... of Because ... plays the ... has ... terror. ... realistic ... Pertwoe ... ics' fears ... overstepped

... after being ... the character ... is the only ... layed by any

The serial was ... when it began, ..." Mr. Pertwoe ... 75 per cent

... is getting more ... children? After

Youngsters can't help liking Jon Pertwee. But little Edward, left, isn't too sure about other 'beings' in the show

all, they are the ones most likely to be watching TV on Saturdays between six and seven in the evening.

A BBC spokesman said: "Dr. Who is not a children's entertainment. We regard it as family entertainment.

"Why, then, did they put the programme on during 'children's hour' in the first place? "Because no child is likely to be watching without parents there," said the BBC man.

One of the autograph hunters who crowded round him later was four-year-old Edward, whose father is a sword-carrying soldier in Horse Guards' Parade, London.

"Do you watch the programme?" Mr. Pertwee asked.

"Sometimes," Edward replied, "but mummy doesn't like us to see it. She says it isn't a nice programme."

Mr. Pertwee, unshaken, said: "What do you remember about the episodes you have seen?" "The Daleks," Edward replied. "I liked them."

One of the reasons the BBC has

Mr. Pertwee told me, at Aldbourne, Wilts, during filming of a black magic episode with the latest of his marvellous monsters: "Parents have the right to. I cannot see that the programme offends children. I'm a parent myself. If I thought my children ought not to see it I wouldn't let them."

### Doesn't care

made *Dr. Who* so terrifying, apparently, is that it goes out on Saturday at teatime. Guaranteed several million viewers each week, the corporation has the chance to hold its large audience for later programmes.

But does the BBC care who it offends?

"No," said Mr. Pertwee. "If people feel the show is too much for them there is a little knob on their TV set. They needn't watch. They can switch off."

But if nobody watches, Dr. Who will kill himself.

A flat-nosed Silurian in 'Dr. Who'

*Agon ... faceless and horrific

A sharp-toothed 'dragon' is no less fierce than an Alien priest

The Primitives ... lined and hard

THESE FIVE PICTURES BY COURTESY OF THE BBC

Jacket painting by John Geary (1980) for W. H. Allen's re-issue of *Doctor Who and the Claws of Axos* by Terrance Dicks (1977, Wyndham Publications Ltd and Allan Wingate (Publishers) Ltd).

exchange for his freedom, but the Doctor traps Axos in a time loop. Realising that the Doctor can be of use to them, the Time Lords send him to the planet Uxarieus where the livelihood of a group of colonists is threatened by a mining corporation. An adjudicator is called in but he turns out to be the Master, who is after an ancient doomsday weapon stored on the planet. The Doctor convinces the alien guardian of the weapon to destroy it. Back on Earth, the Master makes another attempt to gain power for himself by summoning Azal, the last of the alien Dæmons. Azal must pass his power on, but Jo's offering of herself as sacrifice in the Doctor's place causes the Dæmon to have a mental breakdown and destroy himself. The Master is captured by UNIT, bringing his reign of terror to a temporary end.

Above: The Cloven Hoof pub sign (*The Daemons*). Below: Five of the six badges given away free in boxes of Sugar Smacks. The sixth badge was the UNIT emblem (May 1971).

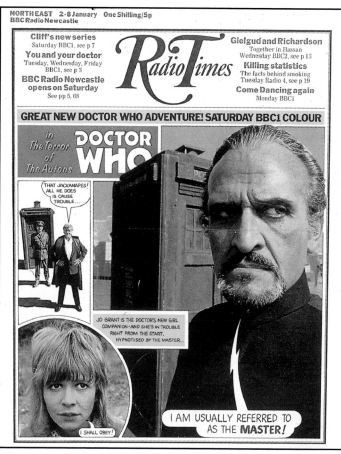

GREAT NEW DOCTOR WHO ADVENTURE! SATURDAY BBC1 COLOUR

St. Michael's Church
Aldbourne

PRICE 5p

There was a crackle of energy and Jo went rigid, her eyes staring before her. The Doctor struggled wildly, but he was firmly held. Helplessly he watched as wrinkles and cracks appeared in Jo's face. Her skin sagged, her hair went first grey, then white ... her body twisted into a crouch. It was like watching a speeded-up film of the effect of the passing years. Jo looked thirty, forty, fifty, sixty, seventy ... she was turning into a wizened old woman before his eyes. Soon she would be dead.

From the novelisation by Terrance Dicks (1977)

Top Left: The arrival of the Master makes the front cover of the *Radio Times* (January 1971). Middle Left: Aldbourne's parish church is used as the main location for *The Daemons* which also features Azal (Stephen Thorne) (May 1971). Left: The Doctor is attacked by a mining robot (*Colony in Space* April 1971).

Jacket painting by Jeff Cummins (1979) for W. H. Allen's re-issue of *Doctor Who and the Doomsday Weapon* by Malcolm Hulke (1974, Universal-Tandem Publishing Co. Ltd).

# Season Nine

Ghosts bring the Doctor to the country home of diplomat Sir Reginald Styles, where he finds travellers from Earth's future who want to kill Styles and thus prevent a war which will result in a Dalek invasion. The Doctor realises that killing Styles caused the war and the rebels are trapped in a temporal paradox. He helps them to resolve it and prevent the Dalek invasion from taking place. The Time Lords redirect the TARDIS to Peladon, a planet hoping to join the Galactic Federation. The Doctor assumes the role of Earth Chairman in the discussions and, aided by the Ice Warrior delegate Izlyr, uncovers a plot between the delegate from Arcturus and the Peladonian High Priest to sabotage the conference.

**WHO IS THE DOCTOR**
**Jon Pertwee**
**PUR III**

Jon Pertwee and the theme music of "Dr. Who" known to millions of viewers. Arrangement, production and special lyrics by Purple's Rupert Hine and David MacIver.

**Press cutting advertising Jon Pertwee's *Doctor Who* related single (December 1972).**

## Magic Moments

*Day of the Daleks* (1972)

The Controller saw the Doctor's face distort with the effort of his mental resistance. But it was in vain. Slowly the first face disappeared and a second one took its place. This showed a younger, dark-haired man with a humorous, rather comic face. 'That is also the Doc-tor.' The voice of the Black Dalek rose to a shriek of triumph. 'You are the Doc-tor. You are an enemy of the Daleks! Now you are in our power! You will be exterminated! YOU WILL BE EXTERMINATED! YOU WILL BE EXTERMINATED!'

Every Dalek in the room aimed its gun-stick at the Doctor's helpless form.

From the novelisation by Terrance Dicks (1974)

**Top Left: The Doctor battles the Ogrons (*Day of the Daleks* January 1972). Centre Left: Jo Grant (Katy Manning), Alpha Centauri (Stuart Fell) and Izlyr (Alan Bennion) attend the conference on Peladon (*The Curse of Peladon* January 1972). Bottom Left: Producer Barry Letts and Jon Pertwee talk about *Doctor Who* at London's Planetarium (December 1971). Bottom Right: The Doctor gets to grips with a Sea Devil (*The Sea Devils* February 1972).**

Jacket painting by Chris Achilleos (1974) for *Doctor Who and the Curse of Peladon* by Brian Hayles (1974, Universal-Tandem Publishing Co. Ltd).

The four jacket paintings for *Doctor Who - The Three Doctors* by Terrance Dicks. Left to Right: Chris Achilleos (1975, Tandem Publishing Ltd), Jeff Cummins (1979, W. H. Allen & Co. Ltd), Alistair Pearson/Alistrations (only used on the BBC Video release in 1991), Alistair Pearson/Alistrations (1991, Virgin Publishing Ltd).

Back on Earth, the Master is using his captivity to summon from the sea intelligent reptiles – cousins of those discovered under Wenley Moor – in an attempt to start a war between them and the humans. He nearly succeeds, but the Doctor intervenes and the Navy bombs the reptiles' underwater base. On the distant planet of Solos in the thirtieth century, experiments are underway to make the surface inhabitable for humans, but this will kill the indigenous population who are starting to mutate into horrific insect creatures. The Doctor, on another mission for the Time Lords, discovers that the mutations are a part of the Solonians' natural life cycle. Back on Earth, the Master makes another attempt to gain power by trying to obtain from Atlantis a crystal with which he can control Kronos the Chronovore and therefore time itself. The Doctor traps the Master in a temporal stalemate and frees Kronos who releases the Time Lords to go their separate ways.

## Magic Moments

### The Sea Devils (1972)

At first Trenchard thought he was seeing things. Was it some kind of seaweed just under the surface, or fish? Then the heads of six Sea-Devils emerged from the water – huge lizards that walked upright like men as they came in from the sea. Each was armed with some strange gadget that resembled a gun.

From the novelisation by Malcolm Hulke (1974)

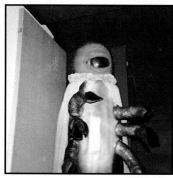

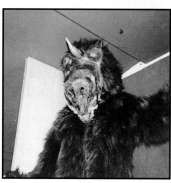

**Top Left:** The *Doctor Who* Fan Club is launched (January 1972). **Bottom Left:** Three photographs from an exhibition at the Ceylon Tea Centre in London mounted to publicise the winners of the *Radio Times* competition. Top to Bottom: Arcturus; Alpha Centauri; Aggedor (all from *The Curse of Peladon*) (March 1972) RMD. **Above:** The Doctor tries to avoid the attentions of his deadliest foes (*The Day of the Daleks* January 1972). **Top Right:** The *Radio Times* features Daleks on its cover and launches a competition to win a Dalek (January 1972).

**Above Left to Bottom:** The Doctor encounters a Solonian mutant (*The Mutants* April 1972). The seventh *Doctor Who* annual (September 1972). The Master (Roger Delgado) seduces Queen Galleia (Ingrid Pitt) (*The Time Monster* May 1972).

**Jacket painting by Jeff Cummins (1977) for *Doctor Who - The Mutants* by Terrance Dicks (1977, Wyndham Publications Ltd and Allan Wingate (Publishers) Ltd).**

# Season Ten

The Time Lords have a problem: their energy is being drained away through a black hole. They summon the Doctor, who, aided by his two previous incarnations, discovers the cause to be Omega, a solar engineer who created the power source which made time travel possible. Omega is trapped in an anti-matter world and wants revenge. The Doctors escape and destroy Omega's domain, turning the black hole into a supernova. The Doctor is returned control of his TARDIS in thanks for helping the Time Lords, and on his first trip in the machine becomes trapped inside a miniaturised menagerie on the planet Inter Minor, where he battles monstrous Drashigs before escaping. On its next journey, the TARDIS

**Left: The *Radio Times* celebrates *Doctor Who*'s tenth anniversary (December 1972). Top to Bottom: Omega (Stephen Thorne) threatens the Time Lords (*The Three Doctors* December 1972). The Doctor, Jo (Katy Manning) and Professor Clifford Jones (Stuart Bevan) (*The Green Death* May 1973). A BBC TV visual effects exhibition at London's Science Museum gives attendees the chance to become a 'TARDIS Commander' (December 1972). The eighth *Doctor Who* annual (September 1973).**

## Magic Moments

***Frontier In Space* (1973)**

**The Master suddenly stepped out from behind a boulder a few yards ahead of the party. 'Hello, Doctor! There you are at long last!'**

**General Williams raised an arm to halt his party. 'Surrender or you will be shot down!' He aimed his blaster gun to fire.**

**'No!' said the Doctor. 'He's unarmed.'**

**'Thank you, Doctor,' called the Master. 'Always the good pacifist. I am unarmed, but not alone. I've brought some old friends along to meet you.'**

**As he spoke a Dalek glided out from behind the boulder, its deadly firing weapon trained on the Doctor.**

**From the novelisation by Malcolm Hulke (1976)**

TARGET

The first three books in the Target range of paperback *Doctor Who* novels are published: *Doctor Who and the Daleks*, *Doctor Who and the Zarbi* and *Doctor Who and the Crusaders* (3 May 1973).

Jacket painting by Chris Achilleos (1976) for *Doctor Who and the Space War* by Malcolm Hulke (1976, Wyndham Publications Ltd and Allan Wingate (Publishers) Ltd).

## Magic Moments

*The Three Doctors (1973)*

Both Doctors turned towards the screen. At the sight of the face they seemed literally dumbstruck, as if someone had turned off their voices. The fierce old man on the screen surveyed them for a moment. It was obvious that somehow he could see them – and he wasn't very impressed. 'So you're what I have become, are you? A dandy and a clown!'

The two Doctors stood before the screen like guilty schoolboys sent to the headmaster, not daring to reply.

From the novelisation by Terrance Dicks (1975)

nearly crashes into a space freighter in the year 2540, bringing the Doctor into the middle of a delicate political stalemate between Earth and Draconia. The sides are on the brink of war when the Doctor discovers that a third party has been manipulating events. This is the Master, who is working with the Daleks. The Doctor sends a telepathic message to the Time Lords to send him after the Daleks. He arrives on the planet Spiridon where he helps a task force of Thals entomb the main Dalek invasion force in ice. Returning to Earth, the Doctor, with the help of a group of environmentalists, prevents an invasion of pollution-fed giant maggots and discovers its cause to be a computer called BOSS. The Doctor convinces the computer's human slave to rebel and destroy the maniacal machine. Jo Grant leaves the Doctor to marry one of the environmentalists.

## Magic Moments

*The Green Death (1973)*

He got out of the bedroom just before a large wet tear cascaded down his 725-year-old cheeks. Slowly he went down the stairs, got into his car Bessie, and drove away.

From the novelisation by Malcolm Hulke (1975)

Top Left: Intergalactic entertainer Vorg (Leslie Dwyer) and his assistant Shirna (Cheryl Hall) contemplate the loss of their livelihood as their Mini-Scope is destroyed (*Carnival of Monsters* January 1973). Bottom Left: To celebrate *Doctor Who*'s tenth anniversary, the *Radio Times* brought out a special magazine (November 1973).

Jacket painting by Alun Hood (1980) for W. H. Allen's re-issue of *Doctor Who and the Green Death* by Malcolm Hulke (1975, Tandem Publishing Ltd).

# Season Eleven

Several notable scientists have vanished without trace and the Doctor realises that an alien force is at work. In Earth's Middle Ages, a Sontaran officer called Linx is using them to repair his spacecraft. Linx is killed just before his ship lifts off, destroying the castle in which it was secreted. When the Doctor returns himself and Sarah Jane Smith – a journalist who had stowed away in the TARDIS – to present-day Earth, they discover that London has been evacuated due to the appearance of prehistoric dinosaurs on the streets. A misguided scientist plans to roll back time for all but a select group of humanity, so that past mistakes can be eradicated and a new

The Green Cross code ✗ Splink

**Top to Bottom, Left to Right:** The Doctor enjoys a quiet moment with the Sontaran Linx (Kevin Lindsay) (*The Time Warrior* December 1973). The Ice Warriors return (*The Monster of Peladon* March 1974). Visitors to the studio set of *The Monster of Peladon* enjoy a meeting with Alpha Centauri (February 1974). The BBC opens its first permanent *Doctor Who* exhibition on Blackpool's Golden Mile (April 1974). Jon Pertwee stars in a series of road safety television advertisements with the catchphrase SPLINK (1974).

The figure looked round the yard as if making sure that it was alone, then raised its hands and lifted the helmet from its head. The face beneath was something out of a nightmare. The head was huge and round, emerging directly from the massive shoulders. The hairless skull was greenish brown in colour, the eyes small and red. The little nose was a pig-like snout, the mouth long and lipless. It was the face from one of Earth's dark legends, the face of a goblin or a troll.

From the novelisation by Terrance Dicks (1978)

Jacket painting by Chris Achilleos (1976) for *Doctor Who and the Dinosaur Invasion* by Malcolm Hulke (1976, Tandem Publishing Ltd and Allan Wingate (Publishers) Ltd).

golden age begin. The Doctor manages to disable the scientist's time machine. On the way to Florana for a holiday, the TARDIS materialises on Exxilon, where a beacon atop a mysterious city drains all the power. Also on the planet are a group of humans and a group of Daleks, all searching for parrinium, a mineral cure for a virulent space plague. The humans destroy the beacon and blow up the Dalek ship. The TARDIS next arrives in one of the caverns below the Citadel on Peladon. The planet is again the focus of attention as someone is sabotaging the mining of trisilicate. The culprits are revealed to be the Ice Warriors. Returning to Earth, Sarah investigates a Tibetan retreat in the English countryside, only to find herself captured by the giant spiders of Metebelis III. The Doctor confronts the spider leader – the Great One – in her radioactive cave of blue

crystal. The radiation destroys the cells of his body, and when the TARDIS finally returns him to Earth, he regenerates once more.

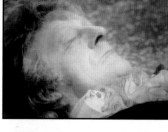

**Top Left: A new season, and Jon Pertwee again graces the cover of the *Radio Times* (December 1973). Bottom Left: The ninth *Doctor Who* annual (September 1974). Above: The Doctor regenerates for the third time (*Planet of the Spiders* May 1974).**

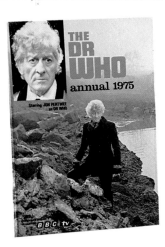

NORTH BBC Radio Humberside
15-21 December 1973 Price 5d

**RadioTimes**

**Who's your friend?**

Page 6: Michael Parkinson, Vanessa Miles and Matthew (son of Paul) Jones say why they'll be turning on to Dr Who, Saturday BBC1 Colour

BBC tv

THE
DR
WHO
annual 1975

Starring JON PERTWEE as DR WHO

BBC

**5.35** *Colour*
**Dr Who**
starring
**Jon Pertwee**
in
*Planet of
the Spiders*
A six-part
story by
**ROBERT SLOMAN**
Part 6
Will **Tommy's** innocence protect him from the power of the spiders? Will the spiders succeed in their plan to take over Earth? Will the Doctor risk destruction by returning to the Cave of the Great One?

| | |
|---|---|
| K'anpo | GEORGE CORMACK |
| Sarah Jane Smith | ELISABETH SLADEN |
| Dr Who | JON PERTWEE |
| Tommy | JOHN KANE |
| Barnes | CHRISTOPHER BURGESS |
| Moss | TERENCE LODGE |
| Keaver | ANDREW STAINES |
| Land | CARL FORGIONE |
| Queen Spider | KISMET DELGADO |
| Cho-je | KEVIN LINDSAY |

**Above Right: Sarah Jane Smith (Elisabeth Sladen) contemplates an eight-legged friend (*Planet of the Spiders*). The *Radio Times* programme listing for part six of *Planet of the Spiders* (8 June 1974).**

## Magic Moments
*The Monster of Peladon (1974)*

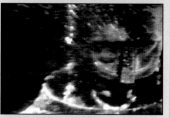

**A terrifying figure stood in the refinery doorway.**

It was immensely tall, covered with green scaly hide that was ridged and plated like that of a crocodile. Its helmet-like head showed a lipless scaly-skinned lower jaw, and its two huge eyes were like blank, black, glass screens. Its huge hands were like crude, powerful clamps. One of them was raised, pointing menacingly at the Doctor. It was an Ice Warrior.

**From the novelisation by Terrance Dicks (1980)**

**The Doctor is surrounded by Daleks on the planet Exxilon (*Death to the Daleks* February 1974).**

Jacket painting by Roy
Knipe/Spectron Artists Ltd
(1978) for *Doctor Who -
Death to the Daleks* by
Terrance Dicks (1978, W.
H. Allen & Co. Ltd).

# Season Twelve

The newly regenerated Doctor is called in by UNIT to help investigate some thefts of components and plans for a secret disintegrator gun. The culprit turns out to be a robot which is being used by a radical group of scientists to hold the world to ransom for a better way of life. The robot is destroyed by a virulent metal virus brewed up by the Doctor. Taking Sarah and his UNIT surgeon Harry Sullivan with him, he leaves in the TARDIS and arrives on a space-station orbiting the Earth in the far future. The station has been invaded by the insect-like Wirrn, and the Doctor helps the humans on board to repel the menace before popping down to Earth to check the alignment of some transmat beacons. Earth too has had visitors. A Sontaran officer, Field Major Styre, has lured some humans to the planet to test human resistance to a Sontaran invasion. The Doctor successfully prevents the Sontarans from invading. The Time Lords hijack the Doctor and his friends when they attempt to return to the TARDIS, and take them to Skaro with instructions to intervene in the development of the Daleks by the brilliant Kaled scientist Davros. The

**Top to Bottom: Tom Baker as the Doctor (1974). An example of Frank Bellamy's superb *Doctor Who* artwork for *Radio Times* (*Genesis of the Daleks* repeat, December 1975). UNIT soldiers battle the Giant Robot (Michael Kilgarriff) (*Robot* December 1974). Press cutting from the *Evening News* 25 January 1975.**

## Magic Moments
### The Ark In Space (1975)

**The Doctor seized Vira's arm and pulled her behind him. He then spoke rapidly to Noah. 'Tell us one thing, Noah. How much time do we have?'**

**Slowly Noah turned his head fully towards them. The whole of the left side of his face was transformed into a shapeless, suppurating mass of glistening green tissue, in the midst of which his eye rolled like an enormous shelled egg. As they stared at him horrified they could almost detect the spreading movement of the alien skin.**

**From the novelisation by Ian Marter (1977)**

**Cover for** *Doctor Who and the Giant Robot* **by Terrance Dicks. Illustration by Peter Brooks (1975, Universal-Tandem Publishing Co. Ltd).**

Doctor tries his best, but history is ultimately changed only marginally. The time travellers return to the space-station, but to a different time, and become involved in a scheme by the Cybermen to destroy Voga – a new moon of Jupiter which has large deposits of gold, a metal lethal to the silver giants. The Cybermen are destroyed by a Vogan rocket and the time travellers leave in the TARDIS to answer a call for help from the Brigadier.

**Above: The Doctor and Sarah (Elisabeth Sladen) examine the dead Wirrn queen (*The Ark in Space* January 1975). Right: Press cutting from the *Daily Express* 25 April 1975.**

**Above: Sarah and Roth (Peter Rutherford) are brought before Sontaran Field Major Styre (Kevin Lindsay) (*The Sontaran Experiment* February 1975).**

**Above: The Doctor and Davros (Michael Wisher), creator of the Daleks (*Genesis of the Daleks* March 1975). Left and Below: Tom Baker arrives at the *Doctor Who* exhibition on Blackpool's Golden Mile and is greeted by a huge crowd (October 1975).**

## *The dotty doctor,*

## hero of 15 million

### By David Wigg

FROM six to sixty, they all loved him . . . the man who brought Dr. Who into the universe.

With his white wig and monocle, the cranky scientist was compulsive viewing to 15 million " children."

But yesterday came the final fade-out for actor William Hartnell, the first man in the " Dr. Who " role, launched on B.B.C. television in 1963. He died in hospital near his home at Marden, Kent, aged 67.

He had been ill for about three years.

Hartnell made a huge success of his science fiction role—predicted to last only six weeks—and completely lost his own identity in it.

**DOCTOR WHO AND THE DALEKS**
**SEVEN KEYS TO DOOMSDAY**

OPENS Mon. Dec.16th 4 weeks ONLY

Performances TWICE DAILY 3.00 & 7.30

Written by Terrance Dicks
Daleks created by Terry Nation
Designed by John Napier
Directed by Mick Hughes

**LIVE...ON... STAGE...**

**A BRAND NEW ADVENTURE**

**ADELPHI** THEATRE TEL.01-836 7611 STRAND.LONDON WC 2

## Magic Moments

***Genesis of the Daleks* (1975)**

'Well he should be finished by now. I'm going to take a look.' A choking cry from inside the room sent them running through the door. In the dim green light, they could see the Doctor swaying wildly. Something like a coating of live black tar was covering his legs, flowing steadily upwards as if to engulf him ...

**From the novelisation by Terrance Dicks (1976)**

**Left: *Doctor Who and the Daleks: Seven Keys to Doomsday* opens at the Adelphi Theatre in London. The play begins with the Doctor (Trevor Martin) regenerating and two members of the audience, Jenny (Wendy Padbury) and Jimmy (James Matthews), stepping forward to help (December 1974).**

Jacket painting by Chris Achilleos (1976) for *Doctor Who and the Genesis of the Daleks* by Terrance Dicks (1976, Tandem Publishing Ltd and Allan Wingate (Publishers) Ltd).

# Season Thirteen

The Doctor has been summoned by the Brigadier to investigate the destruction of several oil rigs off Scotland's coast. The rigs are being attacked by the Skarasen, the cyborg 'pet' of the alien Zygons living at the bottom of Loch Ness. The Zygon spaceship is destroyed and their leader Broton shot by UNIT troops. The Doctor and Sarah take the TARDIS back to London but are drawn off course by a distress signal from the planet Zeta Minor in the year 37166. A Morestran research team has been killed and the Doctor is blamed. The real culprit is an anti-matter force which is preventing the Morestrans from leaving while they have anti-matter on board. The Morestran ship is overrun by

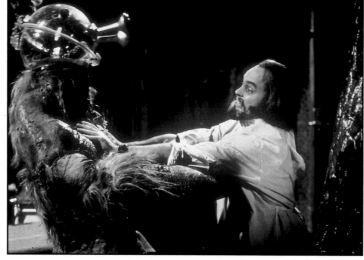

Top Left: Broton (John Woodnutt), leader of the Zygons (*Terror of the Zygons* August 1975). Top Right: Sarah (Elisabeth Sladen) and a disguised Doctor (*Pyramids of Mars* October 1975). Above: Solon (Philip Madoc) struggles with the body he has created to house Morbius' brain (*The Brain of Morbius* January 1976). Left: Weetabix promotes *Doctor Who* by giving away stand-up figures from the series (1975).

Above: *Doctor Who* appears on vinyl in an original story written by Victor Pemberton (1976).

Jacket painting by Chris Achilleos (1976) for *Doctor Who and the Loch Ness Monster* by Terrance Dicks (1976, Tandem Publishing Ltd and Allan Wingate (Publishers) Ltd).

primordial anti-man creatures until the Doctor returns the anti-matter to its rightful dimension. The TARDIS next arrives on Earth in 1911 where the ancient Egyptian god Sutekh is plotting to lay waste to mankind. The Doctor manages to trap the creature in a space/time tunnel where Sutekh dies of old age. Back on what they presume to be present day Earth, Sarah and the Doctor uncover a plot by the alien Kraals to invade the Earth using android duplicates and a simulated Earth village on their own planet Oseidon. They travel to Earth and alert UNIT before the invasion can succeed. The TARDIS is drawn off course by the Time Lords and arrives on Karn, where a scientist named Solon plans to resurrect an evil Time Lord named Morbius by building a new body for Morbius's living brain. The Doctor defeats Morbius in a mind battle and the patchwork creature falls to its death from a mountaintop. Back on Earth, two seed pods are discovered in the Antarctic. These are from a Krynoid, a hostile form of life that engulfs a planet and destroys all animal life there before seeding itself into space. A pod is germinated by an insane botanist but UNIT destroys the resultant creature.

The Doctor and Sarah (Elisabeth Sladen) discover that there is a mysterious force at work on Zeta Minor (*Planet of Evil* September 1975).

The Kraal leader, Styggron (Martin Friend), and his scientist, Chedaki (Roy Skelton), plot to destroy humanity (*The Android Invasion* November 1975).

Left: The tenth *Doctor Who* annual (September 1975). Above: The White Lion hardback edition of the William Hartnell story *The Zarbi*. Strangely, the cover shows the fourth Doctor (Tom Baker) (1975).

The *Doctor Who* Appreciation Society (DWAS) is formed and they release the first edition of their newsletter, *The Celestial Toyroom* (May 1976)

## Magic Moments

*The Android Invasion* (1975)

'Where's the real Sarah? What have you done with her? *Answer me!*'
  The Android broke free, tripped, and cannoned into the trunk of the nearest tree, hitting its head on the trunk. Horrifyingly, its 'Sarah' face was jolted loose, rolling away across the ground. The Doctor looked down at the collapsed android. Packed into the skull cavity was a maze of wire and miniaturised transistors.

From the novelisation by Terrance Dicks (1978)

Jacket painting by Roy
Knipe/Spectron Artists Ltd
(1978) for *Doctor Who and
the Android Invasion* by
Terrance Dicks (1978, W.
H. Allen & Co. Ltd).

# Season Fourteen

**S**ome Mandragora energy hitches a lift in the TARDIS to fifteenth century Earth where it makes contact with Hieronymous, the leader of a religious cult. Mandragora plans to establish itself on Earth but is thwarted by the Doctor, who drains away its power. Upon their return to near-future Earth, Sarah becomes possessed by forces from a ring on a disembodied alien hand which eventually grows into Eldrad, a silicon creature from Kastria. The Doctor returns Eldrad to Kastria, now a dead world, and when the creature plans to rule Earth instead, the Doctor trips him into a crevasse. The Doctor receives a call from Gallifrey, his home planet. He must go there and, as he cannot take Sarah with him, he drops her off on Earth. When he arrives on Gallifrey he is framed for the murder of the President by the Master, who is seeking power to regenerate his body. The Doctor clears

THE AMAZING WORLD OF DOCTOR WHO FREE SPACE-AGE CARDS TO COLLECT

**THE AMAZING WORLD OF DOCTOR WHO**

Explore the Amazing World of Doctor Who with this unique collection of space-age shaped picture cards. Collect colourful pictures of exciting and mysterious characters encountered during the timeless travels of the Tardis.

Look out for the Daleks, Sarah Jane Smith and, of course, the amazing Doctor himself. There are 12 octagonal cards to collect—you'll find one card in each 36 pack, two in a 72 and four in a 144.

UNIQUE DOCTOR WHO BOOK WITH WALLCHART

Here's a very special offer for all Doctor Who fans, young and old! This colourful 64-page book has been created exclusively for Ty Phoo – you cannot buy it anywhere else.

The Amazing World of Doctor Who book contains stories, pictures, and games featuring all the main Doctor Who characters, and comes complete with a colourful 76 x 50 cm wallchart on which you can stick your picture cards. It's yours for just £1 including postage and packing.

Complete the Application Form on the side. If you would like to receive the wallchart alone, send just 20p. It's an offer that's out of this world.

## LEELA CAUSES A STIR

★ **IS SEX** about to rear its irrepressible head in that most adult of children's shows, Dr Who?

I'm getting worried about the doctor's attitude to his new assistant, Leela (Louise Jameson). It does not fit the pattern.

### DISHY

The first doctor, played by William Hartnell, was positively grandfatherly towards his young companions.

The second, Patrick Throughton, was far too tetchy to be bothered with such things.

The third, Jon Pertwee,

was a stylish, but somewhat sexless, soul.

But the present Doctor, Tom Baker, is definitely on the dishy side. And while he was purely avuncular towards silly Sarah, he seems to see Leela in a different light.

I'm sure I detect the stirrings of something sexual. Perhaps he is turned on by the washleather the strange little creature wears on her bum.

But this being a children's show, there won't be any hanky panky, I presume. So will it be Dr and Mrs Who?

Top Left: Sarah (Elisabeth Sladen) with the fossilised alien hand (*The Hand of Fear* October 1976). Top Right: Leela (Louise Jameson) in fighting pose (*The Face of Evil* January 1977). Above: Ty-Phoo Tea's *Doctor Who* promotion featuring free cards, a poster and a book (1976).

At the sight of what lay beneath the mask, Leela froze in horror. Greel's face was warped, distorted, bent, eyes, nose and mouth jumbled nightmarishly together, like a plasticine face squashed by a fist. Leela had only a moment to take in the terrible sight. The pad came down over her face, and she sank into unconsciousness.

From the novelisation by Terrance Dicks (1977)

The first ever *Doctor Who* documentary is transmitted. *Whose Doctor Who* is part of *The Lively Arts* series of programmes presented by Melvyn Bragg (3 April 1977).

**Jacket painting by Roy Knipe/Spectron Artists Ltd (1979) for *Doctor Who and the Hand of Fear* by Terrance Dicks (1979, W. H. Allen & Co. Ltd).**

himself, but the Master escapes to fight again. The TARDIS next arrives on a planet where two groups of humanoids have been fighting for centuries. The Doctor discovers that the controlling computer, Xoanon, has developed a split personality thanks to the Doctor's own meddling in the past, and it is this which is perpetuating the fighting. He erases all but one of the personalities and peace comes to the planet. Leela, one of the savages, goes with the Doctor when he leaves. Their first port of call is a Sandminer, combing a desert planet for precious ores. The robots on the mine are being reprogrammed by Taran Capel to kill the human crew. Capel is ultimately strangled by his own robots. In Victorian London the Doctor and Leela encounter Magnus Greel, a war criminal from the fifty-first century, who is draining young girls of life essence in order to stay alive himself. The Doctor tracks Greel to his lair, where the villain is killed by his own machinery.

Kissing the Daleks Goodbye

Katy Manning talks to Tym Manley

Leela (Louise Jameson) senses trouble on the bridge of the robot-controlled Sandminer (*The Robots of Death* January 1977).

In an attempt to throw off her *Doctor Who* image, Katy Manning poses naked for *Girl Illustrated* magazine (1977).

Above Left: The eleventh *Doctor Who* annual (September 1976). Left: The DWAS organises the world's first *Doctor Who* convention (August 1977). Above: The winners of a BBC competition visit the set of *The Deadly Assassin* and meet Tom Baker (August 1976).

Jacket painting by Jeff
Cummins (1978) for
*Doctor Who and the Face
of Evil* by Terrance Dicks
(1978, W. H. Allen & Co.
Ltd).

# Season Fifteen

The TARDIS arrives at a lighthouse on Fang Rock in the early twentieth century. Around the same time, the survivors from a shipwreck and an alien shape-changer also arrive. The alien Rutan kills off the humans until the Doctor kills the Rutan. Travelling in space, the TARDIS is infected by a virus, and the viral nucleus infects the Doctor. The nucleus uses equipment from the TARDIS to grow to macro size and plans to spawn itself across the galaxy, but the Doctor blows up the breeding tanks. By way of thanks, the Doctor is given a robot dog called K-9. Returning to present-day Earth where the operation of a time scanner has brought about a manifestation of the Fendahl – a creature which is death – the Doctor manages to remove the source of power before the Fendahl can establish itself. On Pluto the inhabitants of a megropolis are being taxed into slavery by a powerful Company. The Company's agent on Pluto is an Usurian, whom the Doctor disables through some

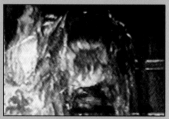

The Fendahl (Wanda Ventham) flanked by one of the Fendahleen (*Image of the Fendahl* October 1977).

Above: Sontaran Commander Stor (Derek Deadman) (*The Invasion of Time* February 1978).

Higsterminate!
Your next pint of Higsons bitter

Hig!

Above: The Doctor and Reuben (Colin Douglas) at the top of the Fang Rock lighthouse (*Horror of Fang Rock* September 1977). Left: Higsons uses a familiar figure to promote their beer. Far Left: The twelfth Doctor Who annual (September 1977).

It was, thought the Doctor dispassionately, quite the nastiest looking life-form he had ever seen. In shape it was vaguely like an immensely thick snake, though the segmented front gave a suggestion of a caterpillar. It was green, and glistening, and it seemed to move on a trail of slime, like a shell-less snail.

The worst thing of all was the mouth. It was large and round, taking up most of the head – there were no eyes – and it was fringed with waving tentacles. From this mouth came a hungry, hissing, gobbling sound, as the creature slid towards them with ghastly deliberation.

From the novelisation by Terrance Dicks (1979)

**Jacket painting by Jeff Cummins (1978) for** *Doctor Who and the Horror of Fang Rock* **by Terrance Dicks (1978, W. H. Allen & Co. Ltd).**

creative accounting. While watching the creation of a new galaxy, the Doctor finds himself drawn into the quest of a group of Minyans to find their lost race banks. The banks are held by a semi-sentient computer, the Oracle, and the Doctor tricks the computer into giving them up. The Vardans want to invade Gallifrey and enrol the Doctor to help them, but the Doctor bluffs them so that he can trap their planet in a time loop. He is unaware that the Vardans are being used by the Sontarans, who want the secret of time travel. The Doctor uses the relics of Rassilon to construct a disintegrator gun and vaporises the Sontaran invaders. While on Gallifrey the Doctor is inaugurated as President of the Time Lords, and Leela falls in love with a guard and stays on Gallifrey with him.

★ WEEKEND WINNER—DR WHO ? (BBC 1, 6.15) : Well, it's still Tom Baker (pictured here with Colin Douglas) —he's got a couple of seasons to go before he catches up with the records set by Jon Pertwee and Patrick Troughton. In this new four-part series by Terrance Dicks he tackles 'The Horror of Fang Rock.' It seems the Tardis is still in England at the turn of the century and the doctor intends to show Leela (Louise Jameson) around Brighton. But when they emerge from the time machine they get quite a surprise. . . .

**Above: A *Doctor Who* spoof appears in *Monster Fun Comic*. Below: K-9, the Doctor's faithful robot dog (*The Invisible Enemy* October 1977).**

**Impressive modelwork by BBC visual effects designer Mat Irvine (*The Invisible Enemy*).**

**The Doctor and Leela on the bridge of the P7E (*Underworld* January 1978).**

## Magic Moments

*The Invasion of Time* (1978)

The Doctor turned.

Three strange figures stood in the doorway, watching him. Not the vanquished Vardans, but three very different figures.

They wore shining space armour. They were short and squat with immensely wide shoulders, broad powerful limbs, and great dome-shaped helmets.

The leader of the three figures removed his helmet to reveal a face from some ancient nightmare.

From the novelisation by Terrance Dicks (1980)

Jacket painting by Roy Knipe/Spectron Artists Ltd (1979) for *Doctor Who and the Invisible Enemy* by Terrance Dicks (1979, W. H. Allen & Co. Ltd).

# Season Sixteen

## Magic Moments
### The Ribos Operation (1978)

T he Doctor is temporarily taken out of time by the White Guardian and then sent on a quest to locate the six segments of the Key to Time. He is joined by Romana, another Time Lord. The first segment is on the planet Ribos, where a conman named Garron is attempting to sell the planet to the Graff Vynda-K. The sale fails and the Doctor retrieves the key, disguised as a nugget of the precious mineral Jethryk. The second segment of the Key to Time

The Doctor and Romana (Mary Tamm) arrive on the icy planet Ribos (*The Ribos Operation* September 1978).

The Pirate Captain (Bruce Purchase) (*The Pirate Planet* September 1978).

Above: Romana is trapped in the stone circle by Miss Fay (Susan Engel) (*The Stones of Blood* October 1978).

Unstoffe put his hand gently on the old man's withered arm. 'One day – in the future – you will be something again,' he said. 'All that you say is true. There are other suns and other worlds ...'

'You ... you believe it, too?' Binro breathed, his eyes suddenly brimming with tears.

Unstoffe put both his hands on Binro's fleshless shoulders. 'I know it is true,' he said. 'I come from one of those other worlds. I promise you, Binro, one day your people will turn to each other and say, "Binro was right. He told the truth." '

From the novelisation by Ian Marter (1979)

Mary Tamm ... high flying

## DR WHO'S SPACE-MATE

### By Ross Benson

MEET Romana, Dr Who's latest starring partner.

She is lovely Mary Tamm, aged 28, who is to play the doctor's new assistant in the next B.B.C. television series.

After lording it over 13 assistants in the last few years, the space-age male chauvinist may have met his match this time.

Romana is a Time Lord her-self, with a mind of her own and an astronomical I.Q. to go with it. She does not believe in doctor's orders.

Says Mary: "The doctor's other girls were in the background, but I am being given a chance to create a per-sonality."

Producer Graham Williams adds : "Romana is just out of Time Lord academy, but the doctor hasn't been to univer-sity for 500 years.

"He resents being told what to do by a young girl."

**Jacket painting by Andrew Skilleter (1980) for _Doctor Who and the Stones of Blood_ by Terrance Dicks (1980, W. H. Allen & Co Ltd).**

# Season Seventeen

The TARDIS's first randomised journey takes the Doctor and Romana to Skaro where the Daleks are searching for Davros to help them break the stalemate in a war against the robot Movellans. They find Davros, but the Doctor organises the Dalek slaves to revolt and Davros is captured and returned to Earth for trial. The Doctor and Romana take a holiday in Paris in 1979 where Count Scarlioni — one of the time-splintered segments of Scaroth of the Jagaroth — is funding time-travel experiments to enable himself to go back in time and prevent his original from splintering. As this is also the event which brought life to the Earth, the Doctor has to stop him. An ambassador from the planet Tythonus, Erato, has been imprisoned in a pit by the rulers of the planet Chloris so that they might retain their monopoly of

The first issue of *Doctor Who Weekly* is published. Initially edited by Dez Skinn, the magazine reached its two-hundredth issue in 1993 (17 October 1979).

One of the robot Movellans, Agella (Suzanne Danielle), outside the Movellan ship on the planet Skaro (*Destiny of the Daleks* September 1979).

The Doctor, Romana (Lalla Ward) and Duggan (Tom Chadbon) travel back in time hoping to prevent Skaroth from changing the course of Earth's history (*City of Death* September 1979).

## Magic Moments

*City of Death* (1979)

Skaroth's ship lifted smoothly from the surface of the Earth, its legs folding neatly into place underneath it.

Seconds later, Skaroth detected a time disturbance, a ripple. He had misjudged the departure and his ship shuddered as the temporal forces gained in strength.

Without warning, the ship exploded around him, vapourising before his eye. The force of the blast spread out over the planet, scorching the already parched earth, and heating the mud into a boiling soup. Skaroth's last thought as his body was shattered into numerous pieces was of the error he had made.

**Extract by David J. Howe**

**Jacket painting by Steve Kyte (1981) for *Doctor Who and the Creature from the Pit* by David Fisher (1981, W. H. Allen & Co. Ltd).**

The Doctor and Romana join a consignment of sacrifices en route to Skonnos to be given to the Nimon, a race of bull-headed aliens who swarm from planet to planet like locusts. The Doctor stops the latest migration by destroying the reception beacon.

Top Left: A Mandrel runs amok (*Nightmare of Eden* November 1979). Below: Tom Baker and Lalla Ward reprise their roles as the Doctor and Romana in a series of computer advertisements for Australian television. Right: The fourteenth *Doctor Who* annual (September 1979).

metal on the planet. The Doctor discovers that the Tythonians are planning to destroy Chloris in retaliation for Erato's imprisonment and with the help of Erato, the Doctor saves Chloris. Alerted by the merging of two space-craft coming out of hyperspace, the Doctor stumbles on a plot to smuggle an addictive drug called vraxoin onto a pleasure planet. He exposes the smugglers to the authorities.

## DR WHO GOING FRENCH

**Tom Baker**

MON DIEU! Tardis is to whisk Dr. Who off to Gay Paree . . . . for real.

Tom Baker and his glamorous new sidekick Lalla Ward are to go on location in the French capital for an episode in the new series, which starts its new run in September.

"It is the first time we have been on location abroad and we plan to film at the top of the Eiffel Tower along the banks of the River Seine. and at several more famous Paris attractions and beauty spots," said producer Graham Williams, obviously very excited by the prospect.

Above: The Doctor with the fearsome Nimon (*The Horns of Nimon* December 1979).

## Magic Moments

*Destiny of the Daleks* (1979)

Guns blazing, [the Daleks] raked the chamber with a deadly burst of fire. But the chamber was empty. They moved across the room and directed their fire up the shaft...

There was a slithering sound and a coil of rope slid down the shaft and dropped in front of them. The Doctor's voice floated down. 'Think you're the most superior race in the Universe, don't you? Well, just try climbing up after us!'

From the novelisation by Terrance Dicks (1979)

Jacket painting by Steve Kyte (1980) for *Doctor Who and the Horns of Nimon* by Terrance Dicks (1980, W. H. Allen & Co. Ltd).

# THE EIGHTIES

**U**nlike previous decades, in the 1980s Doctor Who had one long-serving producer, John Nathan-Turner. After seven years, Tom Baker decided to leave the series, and his swan-song in *Logopolis* at the end of the eighteenth season left a lump in many people's throats, and much doubt as to whether the programme could survive Baker's departure. His replacement was Peter Davison, already a household name through playing Tristan Farnon in *All Creatures Great and Small*. Davison brought a fresh and energetic approach to the part, and his Doctor once again confronted enemies such as the Daleks and the Cybermen. Although *Doctor Who* lost its traditional Saturday teatime slot and was aired early on weekday evenings, it still managed to pull in respectable audiences, and, with John Nathan-Turner's aptitude for spotting media opportunities, was never short of publicity. Nathan-Turner also became *Doctor Who*'s ambassador to America where the programme was growing in popularity. By the mid-eighties American conventions were being attended by tens of thousands of people, and in 1983, to celebrate *Doctor Who*'s twentieth anniversary, the BBC organised a huge event in England at Longleat House in Wiltshire. Eventually Davison decided to leave, and Nathan-Turner chose Colin Baker to

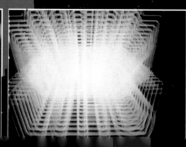

replace him. Baker was known for his portrayal of bad guy Paul Merroney in *The Brothers*, and to try and make the sixth Doctor as different from the fifth as Davison's portrayal was from Tom Baker's, the Doctor was initially made unlikeable, unpredictable and tasteless. After one season the BBC put the programme on hold for eighteen months, citing examples of violence and bad taste in what was still regarded as a children's programme. What the BBC was not prepared for was a media backlash which resulted in Bill Cotton personally telephoning the coordinator of the *Doctor Who* Appreciation Society to assure the fans of the programme's future. The Doctor returned in *The Trial of a Time Lord*, an ambitious fourteen-part story, but following this Colin Baker was unceremoniously sacked and Nathan-Turner was told to introduce yet another Doctor. He chose Sylvester McCoy, a multi-talented and versatile actor. His Doctor echoed the whimsical nature of Patrick Troughton's portrayal and was both likeable and watchable. He was paired with Bonnie Langford's unpopular Mel until she decided to move on, and Sophie Aldred was introduced as the tough, streetwise Ace. Combined with generally more intelligent and thought-provoking scripts, *Doctor Who* continued for another two seasons before the BBC again pulled the plug – this time for no apparent reason. At the time it was cancelled, *Doctor Who* was once more increasing in popularity and sales of all merchandise, in particular the BBC videos, were proving that there was still a large audience for *Doctor Who*.

# Season Eighteen

The Doctor, Romana and a broken K-9 head for a holiday on the planet Argolis in the year 2290, only to find that it is under attack from the reptilian Foamasi. The Doctor prevents one of the Argolins from creating an army of clones and leaves as the Foamasi start discussions with the Argolins about their future. En route to the planet Tigella, the TARDIS is trapped in a time loop by Meglos, last of the Zolfa-Thurans, who then impersonates the Doctor in order to steal the

## Time's up, Doctor

TOM BAKER . . . There's nothing more I can do in the series.

### And the new Who could be a woman

By PAUL DONOVAN

TOM BAKER is quitting as TV's Doctor Who.

And the Time Lord's successor in the BBC science fiction series could be a woman.

Last night Baker denied that an argument with the producer led to his decision.

But he admitted he was upset by the recent demise of K-9, the doctor's mechanical dog.

He said he had argued against writing out K-9. And he claimed producer John Nathan-Turner had not tried to persuade him to stay.

#### Assistant

'There's nothing more I can do in the series except repetition,' said the 46-year-old former building labourer.

He will be seen in his last two episodes with the doctor's new assistant, Janet Fielding.

Mr Nathan-Smith said last night he had asked Baker to stay. He will be announcing the new Dr Who in a month.

'I've spoken to various people, some of them ladies,' he said.

Who's who—Page 17.

**Above:** Press cutting announcing Tom Baker's departure from the series. **Left:** A Foamasi prowls the corridors of the Argolin Leisure Hive (*The Leisure Hive* August 1980).

**The Doctor regenerates for the fourth time (*Logopolis* February 1981).**

**The Doctor with the evil calified Melkur (*The Keeper of Traken* January 1981).**

## Magic Moments

*Full Circle* (1980)

They rose from the waters of the marshland one by one, tall, powerful, scaly creatures, dripping mud and slime. Their clawed hands tore at the air around them as sounds of inhuman ferocity were released from their throats.

They stood erect, sucking in breath, and by the nature of their stance declared that they claimed this territory as their own.

The Doctor tensed. He had nowhere to run.

From the novelisation by Andrew Smith (1982)

KAD

Jacket painting by Alistair
Pearson/Alistrations
(1993) for Virgin
Publishing's re-issue of
*Doctor Who and the
Leisure Hive* by David
Fisher (1982, W. H. Allen
& Co. Ltd).

**5.10 pm
Doctor Who**
starring **Tom Baker**
in *Logopolis*
The final part of a story by
CHRISTOPHER H. BIDMEAD
4: Will the Monitor's program
stave off fate? What is the Distant
Stranger's task? How does the
Time Lords' fatal duel resolve?
Doctor Who..................TOM BAKER
The Master..........ANTHONY AINLEY
The Monitor...............JOHN FRASER
Tegan....................JANET FIELDING
Nyssa.....................SARAH SUTTON
Adric..........MATTHEW WATERHOUSE
Security guard..CHRISTOPHER HURST
Script editor CHRISTOPHER H. BIDMEAD
Designer MALCOLM THORNTON
Executive producer BARRY LETTS
Producer JOHN NATHAN-TURNER
Director PETER GRIMWADE

Tigellan's power source. The
Doctor stops Meglos from
destroying Tigella. The Doctor
receives a message from the
Time Lords, but the TARDIS
slips through a hole in space
and arrives on the planet
Alzarius in E-Space – a
parallel space continuum.
Alzarius is entering another
phase of its seasonal plan-
etary cycle, and the Doctor
helps the Alzarians under-
stand what they are up
against and to escape from
the planet themselves. A
young Alzarian called Adric
stows away on the TARDIS.
Still in E-Space, the TARDIS

arrives on a world ruled by
three vampires. The vampires
want to sacrifice Romana to
the Great Vampire as he
awakes, but the Doctor
stakes the giant creature
through the heart with a
space-ship. The TARDIS
arrives at the intersection of
E-Space and N-Space and the
Doctor helps the time-sensi-
tive Tharils usurp their
enslavers. Romana and K-9
remain to help the Tharils
free the rest of their people.
Returning to N-Space, the
Doctor is contacted by the
Keeper of Traken, who asks
his help in defeating an evil

which has come to his
planet. The evil is the Master,
who takes as his own the
body of Tremas, a Traken
consul. The Master follows
the Doctor to Logopolis where
he interferes with the
Logopolitans' mathematical
calculations and threatens
the very existence of the
universe. The Doctor stabi-
lises the calculations but
falls from a radio-telescope
on Earth and is forced to
regenerate, much to the
astonishment of Adric and his
new companions – Tegan, an
Australian air hostess, and
Nyssa, Tremas's daughter.

Above: Biroc the Tharil (David
Weston) (*Warriors' Gate*
January 1981). Below: The
fifteenth (September 1980) and
sixteenth (September
1981) *Doctor Who* annuals.

'... And whosoever knoweth just cause or impediment'

Top Left: A *Doctor Who* float
appears in the annual Lord
Mayor's parade through the
streets of London (14 November
1981). Left: The Master
(Anthony Ainley) (*Logopolis*
February 1981). Above: A
*Doctor Who* exhibition opens at
London's Madame Tussaudes'
(29 August 1980).

**Jacket painting by Andrew Skilleter (1982) for** *Doctor Who - Logopolis* **by Christopher H. Bidmead (1982, W. H. Allen & Co. Ltd).**

# Season Nineteen

The newly regenerated Doctor is taken back to the TARDIS by Tegan and Nyssa. The Master captures Adric and uses his mathematical skills to create a complex trap for the Doctor. The Doctor realises that the place called Castrovalva is the trap in time to escape. The TARDIS next arrives upon a spaceship travelling towards the Earth. The frog-like Urbankan leader Monarch plans to kill off humanity to make space for his own people, and also wants to travel back in time to meet God. Unlike his crew, Monarch is not an android, and he is killed by the disease with which he had hoped to murder humanity. On the planet Deva Loka a snake-like intelligence called the Mara tries to use Tegan to reincarnate itself but the Doctor traps the creature in a circle of mirrors and returns it to whence it came. Three Terileptils crash-land on Earth in 1666 where they plan to release plague-carrying rats

**Above: Monarch (Stratford Johns) (*Four to Doomsday* January 1982). Below: 'Castrovalva', a lithograph by artist M C Escher (1930), the inspiration for the story of the same name. Bottom: Press cutting from the BBC staff magazine *Ariel* 24 February 1982.**

*"Doing all right for yourself I see, veterinary!"*

**The Doctor contemplates his travels in time and space.**

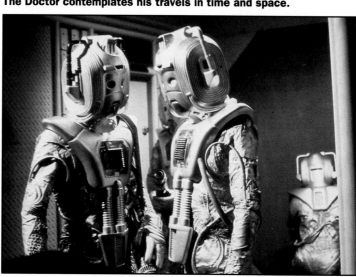

**The Cyberleader (David Banks) attempts to gain control of the space freighter on which the Cybermen are travelling to Earth (*Earthshock* March 1982).**

## Magic Moments

*Kinda* (1982)

The Doctor had accidentally trodden on one of Sanders' little cardboard figures, crushing it. He bent and picked it up.

'I'm so sorry ...'

Hindle snatched it from him, tearing it in the process. 'Now see what you've done!'

Gently Sanders took the figure. 'It's easily mended, you know. A drop of glue ...'

Hindle was sobbing with rage. 'Don't be silly,' he screamed. 'You can't mend people, can you? You can't mend people!'

**From the novelisation by Terrance Dicks (1983)**

**Unused jacket painting by David McAllister (1982) for _Doctor Who and the Visitation_.**

**Cover for _Doctor Who and the Visitation_ by Eric Saward (1982, W. H. Allen & Co. Ltd).**

in London. The Doctor stops them but in doing so accidentally starts a fire in Pudding Lane. Still in England, the Doctor and his friends join a family game of cricket before attending a masked ball in 1925. Nyssa is the double of Ann Talbot, and this causes confusion when Ann's horribly disfigured ex-fiancé kidnaps Nyssa believing her to be Ann, but the Doctor manages to resolve the situation. The TARDIS arrives on Earth in the year 2526 where the Cybermen are planning another invasion. Their

invasion force, hidden on a space freighter, is sent plunging back in time to crash into the Earth, wiping out the dinosaurs and killing Adric who was also on board. The Doctor manages to return Tegan to Earth in her own time, only to become involved in the disappearance of Concorde. The Master has taken the aeroplane back in time, and is using the hypnotised passengers to free the Xeraphin, powerful alien creatures. The Doctor thwarts his plans and traps the Master on Xeraphas.

Above: *Time Out* dated 1-7 January 1982. Below: The original design for the fifth Doctor's costume.

## Dr Who's lad is dead unlucky

DR WHO'S crewmate Adric died trying to save the world last night—and he wasn't too happy about it.

Actor Matthew Waterhouse said : 'I was a bit disappointed and upset.'

Matthew, 20, wanted to be written out of the script but instead became the

**Matthew : Upset**

first main character to die in the show's 19 years.

He perished heroically trying to divert a plummeting spaceship from destroying Earth.

Matthew, of Haywards Heath, Sussex, said : 'Dr Who's companions normally leave by falling in love, or going off to help some under - developed planet—there's never been one of them killed before.'

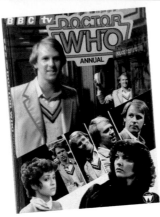

Above Left: Peter Davison, Janet Fielding and Sarah Sutton pose for publicity photographs in their costumes from *Black Orchid* (March 1982). Left: The seventeenth *Doctor Who* annual (September 1982). Below: Press cutting from the *Daily Express* 4 January 1982.

## Magic Moments

*Earthshock (1982)*

The larger of the two figures reached out a bunched metal hand and made a small adjustment to the control module beneath the softly glowing disk. At once the reddish image under the projectors came to rest. The figure's rhythmic breathing paused momentarily and with a faint leathery creak it leaned forward to examine the outline of the mass of rocks. After a slight stirring of inner mechanisms, the figure spoke in a rasping, hollow, mechanical voice.

'They are there. They must be destroyed. Destroyed at once.' The huge hand hovered above a series of triggering buttons and then descended ...

From the novelisation by Ian Marter (1983)

## Everyday problems of the new Time Lord

PETER DAVISON, currently seen each Thursday in the BBC2 repeats of All Creatures Great and Small, makes his debut tonight on BBC1 at 6.55 as the new, youthful "Doctor Who."

But this time the Doctor is not just concerned with the

everyday problems of running the Tardis and being a Time Lord. He has obviously been singled out by BBC1's Controller, Alan Hart, to grab a larger chunk of the early evening, start - of - the - week ratings.

For the first time there will

be two "Doctor Who" episodes a week, on Mondays and Tuesdays. Which should also secure a healthy audience for the new look "Nationwide," now with David Dimbleby at the helm, which goes out immediately beforehand.

Tonight, in the opening

episode of a four-part adventure called "It's Castrolava," the Doctor, Nyssa (Sarah Sutton), Tegan (Janet Fielding) and Adric (Matthew Waterhouse) escape in the Tardis—but within it, there is much confusion among the occupants.

Jacket painting by Alistair Pearson/Alistrations (1992) for Virgin Publishing's re-issue of *Doctor Who - Earthshock* by Ian Marter (1983, W. H. Allen & Co. Ltd).

# Season Twenty

On Earth, Tegan's cousin is captured by Omega, trying once again to gain entry into our universe. Omega plans to use the Doctor's body, but the Doctor destroys him. Tegan, travelling again with the Doctor, dreams of snakes and caves. The Mara is trying to reassert itself and on the planet Manussa it nearly succeeds. The Doctor uses a crystal to focus a calming influence and rob the Mara of power. On an eternally travelling spaceship are Mawdryn and his fellow scientists. Their experiments have given them immortality; now they want the Doctor to use the power of his remaining regenerations to kill them. The Black Guardian has recruited an alien named Turlough to help destroy the Doctor and his meddling with the TARDIS causes it to partially materialise on a ship carrying plague victims to a care centre at Terminus, a giant space station at the centre of the universe. The Doctor realises that a previous explosion at Terminus created the universe, and that a similar explosion will shortly destroy it. He manages to prevent this and Nyssa stays to help care for the plague victims. The Doctor becomes involved in the interplanetary games of the Eternals, timeless and formless beings who are staging a race for the prize of enlightenment. The race is being run by the Guardians who offer the Doctor the prize. He refuses, as does Turlough, and the Black Guardian is defeated again.

## Magic Moments

*Mawdryn Undead (1983)*

The man in the Doctor's red coat turned slowly. Tegan and Nyssa, running in behind the Brigadier, screamed.

The injured creature from the transmat capsule had recuperated amazingly. But he was nothing like the Doctor as any of them had ever known him, with his bulging reptilian eyes, his high domed forehead and slimy flesh that crept and quivered like a stranded fish.

They confronted an alien.

From the novelisation by Peter Grimwade (1983)

To celebrate the twentieth anniversary of *Doctor Who* BBC Enterprises organises a massive convention at Longleat House in Wiltshire over the bank holiday weekend of 3-4 April 1984. Above and Left are the entry ticket and celebration brochure for the event.

The Doctor, watched by Kari (Lisa Goddard), attempts to save the Universe from destruction (*Terminus* February 1983)

**Jacket painting by Alister Pearson with thanks to Jon V Way and Steve Wickham (1992) for Virgin Publishing's re-issue of *Doctor Who - Arc of Infinity* by Terrance Dicks (1983, W. H. Allen & Co. Ltd).**

Arriving on Earth in the year 1215, the Doctor uncovers the Master's plot to use an android replica of King John to prevent the Magna Carta from being signed. The android is Kamelion, a weapon found by the Master on Xeraphas, and the Doctor takes control of it. On Gallifrey, President Borusa is determined to gain eternal life, and intends to use the first five incarnations of the Doctor to traverse the Death Zone and to open Rassilon's tomb for him to gain immortality. Rassilon had prepared for this, and Borusa wins eternal life as a statue.

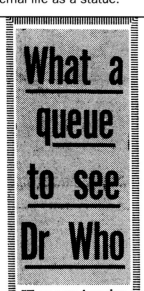

# What a queue to see Dr Who

IT was an invasion so massive that even the great Dr. Who had to admit defeat.

But, in this case, the Doctor was fighting off not an enemy but his friends — 40,000 of them.

The fans flocked to Longleat, Wiltshire, yesterday where a two - day exhibition opened to celebrate the BBC show's 20th anniversary.

But so many Who-addicts turned up that the organisers had to close the gates to non-ticket holders by mid-afternoon.

The present Dr. Who, Peter Davison, went out to chat to the disappointed fans.

Those who did get in could tour film sets and came face to face with Daleks, Cybermen and Ice Warriors.

Some costumes were up for sale—a Cyber-man shirt went for £235.

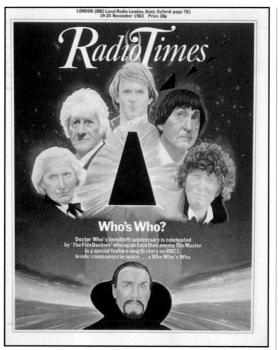

After a break of many years, *Doctor Who* again returns to the cover of the *Radio Times* (November 1983).

Due to popular demand, the *Radio Times* also publishes a special magazine to celebrate the anniversary.

The Doctors meet in the anniversary story (Richard Hurndell, Peter Davison, Jon Pertwee and Patrick Troughton) (*The Five Doctors* November 1983).

The eighteenth *Doctor Who* annual (September 1983).

Left: Press cutting from the *Daily Star* 4 April 1983. Above: The Doctor and Marriner (Christopher Brown) (*Enlightenment* March 1983).

The Doctor discovers the true identity of King Richard. He is an android called Kameleon, controlled by the Master (Anthony Ainley) (*The King's Demons* March 1983).

**Jacket painting by David
McAllister (1986) for
*Doctor Who - The King's
Demons* by Terence Dudley
(1986, W. H. Allen & Co.
Plc).**

# Season Twenty One

On Earth in the year 2084, the reptile race known as the Silurians have woken again, and, with the help of a group of Sea Devil warriors, attack an underwater military base. The Doctor is at hand to prevent a global nuclear war. Tegan wants to visit her grandfather but when they arrive in his home village of Little Hodcombe in 1984, they discover that an alien weapon, the Malus, is stirring up strong feelings in some local war games. The Doctor defuses the situation and the Malus is destroyed. On the planet Frontios an Earth colony is being plagued with disappearances which turn out to be the work of the

## JUST WHAT THE DOCTOR ORDERED!

FANS of *Dr Who* are in no doubt — the Time Lord's latest assistant is the sexiest yet.

Stunning Nicola Bryant, 22, has got the fellas glued to the BBC1 series every Thursday and Friday as she shows off her ample curves in a skimpy bikini and plunging necklines.

But despite her lack of protective clothing, Nicola refused a stand-in for the dangerous scenes.

She has been cut and bruised sliding down a mountainside of sharp volcanic ash, nearly frozen in the Atlantic pretending she was drowning, spent 90 minutes in a smoke-filled cave and been dropped accidentally on her back.

Nicola, who plays Peri Brown, needed frequent treatment for injuries on location and make-up girls had to cover her cuts and bruises with cosmetics.

She says: "I'm so thrilled to be playing the part, but I never knew it would be so painful."

Nicola has been a long-term *Dr Who* fan and set her heart on starring in the show when she was only 12.

"But I could not have imagined my break would come so soon," she says. "I'm straight out of drama school and this is my first acting job."

Peter Davison, who is playing the Doctor for the last time, reckons Nicola is a real tonic. He says: "She is very keen and uses every spare moment learning the business. And she looks more like a James Bond girl than a Dr Who girl.

"Watching her, it's as much as I can do to persuade myself that I am right to leave."

*David Bromfield*

PICTURE BY MIKE WILSON

**Top: Press cutting from *Titbits* 4 February 1984. Centre Left: The nineteenth *Doctor Who* annual (September 1984). Centre: The *Doctor Who* illuminations at Blackpool (Winter 1984) PR. Above: Commander Lytton (Maurice Colbourne) (*Resurrection of the Daleks* February 1984). Left: The Doctor encounters the Malus (*The Awakening* January 1984).**

## Magic Moments

*Resurrection of the Daleks* (1984)

Maybe the shield could take it, thought Styles as she waited to see what would happen. Maybe the Daleks can't get through after all.

With an almighty explosion, the protective air-lock shield shattered under the might of the Daleks' assault. Smoke and shrapnel filled the air as Styles watched the advance guard of Daleks glide onto the ship.

**Extract by David J. Howe**

**Jacket painting by Andrew Skilleter (1984) for _Doctor Who - Planet of Fire_ by Peter Grimwade (1984, W. H. Allen & Co. Plc).**

Tractators, alien creatures which can control gravity. The Doctor removes the intelligent Tractator leader to another planet, and without his controlling influence the nest is rendered harmless. The TARDIS is caught in a time corridor and taken to Earth in 1984. The Daleks plan to use a robot double of the Doctor to infiltrate and kill the high council on Gallifrey. With the help of a rebel Dalek replicant, the Dalek fleet is destroyed, as are the Daleks on Earth. Tegan leaves the Doctor to stay on Earth. An American teenager, Peri, finds an alien beacon whilst on holiday and the Doctor becomes involved in the Master's plan to regain his correct size (he had acciden-

tally been shrunk) by using the restorative powers of a gas on the planet Sarn. The Master is apparently vaporised by the flames. Peri continues to travel with the Doctor and Turlough returns to his home world with his new-found brother. On Androzani Minor, the Doctor and Peri become involved in gun-running, political intrigue and the unwanted attentions of a madman named Sharaz

Jek. Jek is defeated but the Doctor and Peri have contracted spectrox toxaemia and the Doctor can obtain a cure only for Peri, and is forced to regenerate. The new Doctor is unstable, and while trying to find a suitable planet upon which to become a hermit, runs up against the plans of the Gastropod Mestor to spread his eggs through the universe. The Doctor manages to defeat Mestor.

**The Doctor regenerates for the fifth time (*The Caves of Androzani* March 1984).**

**COLIN BAKER**
*Dream role*

# Big hooray for Who from Colin

★ LANDING the role of Dr. Who is a dream come true for former lawyer Colin Baker.

"I have always adored the character", says Colin, who played Paul Merrone in The Brothers.

Colin takes over tonight in THE TWIN DILEMMA (BBC-1, 6.40), a new four-part story which is the last in the present series. He is the sixth actor to play the intrepid doctor.

**Top: Sharaz Jek (Christopher Gable) with his android helpers (*The Caves of Androzani*). Left: Press cutting from the *Daily Mirror* 22 March 1984. Above: The Doctor with genius twins Romulus (Paul Conrad) and Remus (Andrew Conrad) (*The Twin Dilemma* March 1984).**

## Magic Moments

*The Caves of Androzani (1984)*

'I'll give you till a count of three,' screamed Stotz. 'One!'
Quite unperturbed the Doctor went on. 'Unless of course I can find the antidote ...'
'Two!'
'I owe it to my friend Peri to try because I got her into this. So you see, I'm not going to let you stop me now!'
The Doctor closed his eyes.
On the screen, the surface of Androzani Minor rushed closer ...

**From the novelisation by Terrance Dicks (1984)**

Unused jacket painting by Andrew Skilleter (1985) for *Doctor Who - The Twin Dilemma.*

Cover for *Doctor Who - The Twin Dilemma* by Eric Saward. Illustration by Andrew Skilleter (1985, W. H. Allen & Co. Plc).

Jacket painting by Andrew Skilleter (1984) for *Doctor Who - The Caves of Androzani* by Terrance Dicks (1984, W. H. Allen & Co. Plc).

# Season Twenty Two

The Cybermen lure the Doctor to Earth in 1985 where they commandeer the TARDIS to take them to Telos. They intend to pilot Halley's Comet into the Earth, but the Cryons, the original inhabitants of Telos, help the Doctor to destroy the Cybermen's base of operations. The TARDIS runs out of power and the Doctor goes to the planet Varos to obtain supplies of Zyton-7. He becomes involved in the televised torture which is popular there, and also prevents the maggot-like Sil from obtaining the ore at cheap rates. The Master pulls the TARDIS off course to England at the time of the Industrial Revolution. Also on Earth is the Rani, another Time Lord, who is taking brain fluid from humans leaving them aggressive and restless. The Doctor prevents the Master and the

**Peri (Nicola Bryant) wonders what fate has in store for her (*The Two Doctors* February 1985).**

**The second Doctor (*The Two Doctors*).**

*"... wait don't tell me ... I never forget a face ..."*

**Above: Cartoon from the *Daily Mail* 1 March 1985 on the postponement of *Doctor Who* for eighteen months. Far Left: Press cutting from the Sun 28 February 1985. Left: Sontaran Group Marshal Stike (Clinton Greyn) (*The Two Doctors*).**

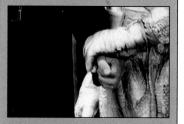

Jacket painting by Colin Howard (1989) for *Doctor Who - Attack of the Cybermen* by Eric Saward (1989, W. H. Allen & Co. Plc).

Rani from interfering in Earth's development. The Doctor becomes involved when a mission his second incarnation was sent on by the Time Lords goes wrong. The second Doctor has been captured by the Sontarans, who want the secret of time travel, but their allegiance with the augmented Androgum Chessene falls apart and the Doctor escapes with both his lives. The operation of another time corridor brings the Doctor to Karfel where the inhabitants live in fear of the Borad, their dictator. The Borad plans to kill off his people and

Above: Golden Wonder run a *Doctor Who* promotion on their bags of crisps and snacks (1986). Top Right: The *Daily Star* gives away stickers when *Doctor Who* is postponed (March 1985).

repopulate the planet with creatures like himself – half-human, half-reptilian Morlox. The Doctor thwarts him and negotiates a peace with the neighbouring Bandrils, whom the Borad was intending to use to wipe out the Karfelons. The Doctor decides to pay his respects to the body of an old friend on the planet Necros. He stumbles into a trap set by Davros, who is running a mortuary facility on the planet and is using the bodies to create new Daleks. Davros is captured by Imperial Daleks and his own Daleks are defeated.

## Magic Moments

*Revelation of the Daleks* (1985)

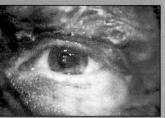

Above: One of the Borad's androids (Dean Hollingsworth) (*Timelash* March 1985). Below: The Doctor makes an appearance on *Jim'll Fix It* (February 1985).

The Master (Anthony Ainley) and the Rani (Kate O'Mara) plot to kill the Doctor (*The Mark of the Rani* February 1985).

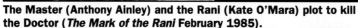

Left: The twentieth, and final, *Doctor Who* annual (September 1985). Above: The Doctor finds himself up against Davros (Terry Molloy) (*Revelation of the Daleks* March 1985).

It was a Dalek, but unlike any that Grigory had seen before. Light glinted off its multifaceted surfaces and pulsed in time with the throbbing sound from the incubators. Within the transparent glass-like shell could be seen the Dalek creature itself: a mass of red raw tissue and nerves. Fluids were clearly visible in the pumping veins and its vestigial limbs twitched as it was nourished.

As Grigory looked, he suddenly realised what was inside the clear casing - it was the remains of a human head. As if by an unspoken command, a single eye flicked open in the ruined face and looked straight at him.

Extract by David J. Howe

**Jacket painting by David McAllister (1985) for *Doctor Who - Timelash* by Glen McCoy (1985, W. H. Allen & Co. Plc).**

# Season Twenty Three

The Doctor is put on trial by the Time Lords. The Valeyard is prosecuting and he presents two recent examples of the Doctor's behaviour to the court. First is the Doctor's action in helping to free the population of the planet Ravalox from the rule of a robot named Drathro, who is guarding some secrets brought by three sleepers from Andromeda. Ravalox turns out to be Earth, moved across the galaxy by persons, and for reasons, unknown. The next evidence comes from the Doctor's visit to the planet Thoros-Beta where Kiv, the leader of the alien Mentors whose number include Sil, is looking for a new body to house his intelligence. Peri is chosen and the Doctor is taken out of time to stand trial before he can help her. She is apparently killed. The Doctor presents his defence, an adventure from his future when he and his companion

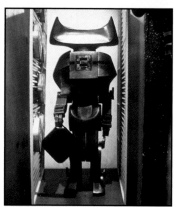

Above: The Valeyard (Michael Jayston), an amalgamation of the Doctor's darker side (*The Trial of a Time Lord* September 1986). Left: Drathro (*The Trial of a Time Lord*). Below: Press cutting from *The Times* 30 March 1987.

## MR PATRICK TROUGHTON

Mr Patrick Troughton, best known for his flamboyant portrayal of Dr Who in the BBC's science fiction children's series of that name, died suddenly on March 28. He was 67.

Born Patrick George Troughton on March 25, 1920, he was educated at Mill Hill School, north London.

He then trained at the Embassy School of Acting and won a scholarship to Leighton Rollin's Studio for Actors at Long Island, New York.

After war service at sea he joined the Bristol Old Vic and became a Shakespearean actor. He also played Hitler in the Gateway Theatre production of *Eva Braun* in 1950.

Troughton went on to become a familiar face on television, appearing in *The Six Wives of Henry VIII*, *Family at War*, *Dr Finlay's Casebook*

and *Colditz*. He always turned in a competent performance.

In 1966 he became the second Dr Who in succession to William Hartnell, and brought his own natural sense of fun to his encounters with the exterminating Daleks. He played the part for three years.

His film credits included *Frankenstein*, *Sinbad and the Tiger* and *The Omen*.

Golf occupied some of his time, so did sailing; and he was a talented amateur painter.

Troughton, who was thrice married, leaves a widow, Shelagh, four sons, two daughters, a stepson and a stepdaughter.

Jacket painting by Tony Masero (1987) for *Doctor Who - The Mysterious Planet* by Terrance Dicks (1987, W. H. Allen & Co. Plc).

Mel save the passengers on a space liner from being killed by the Vervoids, a hostile plant species. The Valeyard twists the Doctor's defence and accuses him of genocide of the Vervoid race. The Doctor suspects that the Matrix evidence has been tampered with and the Master appears to verify the Doctor's claim. The Valeyard turns out to be a future interim incarnation of the Doctor who is planning to kill the Council of Time Lords. The Doctor prevents him and all charges against the Doctor are dropped. Mel, who came to the court to defend the Doctor, travels on with him and it is revealed that Peri did not die but instead got married to a Warlord from Krontep.

## Dr Who actor runs out of time

DR WHO star Colin Baker angrily ended his space travels yesterday.

He resigned from his starring role, after BBC chiefs warned that they were preparing to replace him during the next series.

They had decided that the famous Time Lord needed a new face and were only ready to offer 41-year-old Baker four episodes in the new series to be filmed next spring.

The outraged star, who rose to fame in TV's The Brothers, chose to resign immediately. His agent Barry Burnett said last night. 'Colin is sorry and disappointed to be leaving a part he loved.

The six-week period it would take to film the four episodes at the end of March is a vital time for casting major stage and television shows, and the actor did not want to miss the opportunity to find fresh work.

Baker, the sixth Dr Who, joined the cult sci-fi series in 1983.

**Above: Press cutting from the *Daily Mail* 19 December 1986. Right: Jon Pertwee and friends arrive at London's Virgin Megastore to sign copies of the new BBC Video *Death to the Daleks* (August 1987) AC. Far Right: The BBC sends a massive mobile *Doctor Who* exhibition to tour America (May 1986).**

Mel (Bonnie Langford) and the Doctor on board the *Hyperion III* (*The Trial of a Time Lord* September 1986).

A Vervoid (*The Trial of a Time Lord*).

Colin Baker gets stuck into the part of the Doctor as members of the production crew look on (*The Trial of a Time Lord*).

## Magic Moments

*The Trial of a Time Lord* (13-14) (1986)

A mistake.
  In bending, he lost his balance ...
  And fell flat on his back ...
  In the muddy pool of quicksand ...
  'Goodbye, Doctor,' the Valeyard called.
  Goodbye it seemed indeed. The Doctor's torso ... neck ... then curly head sank beneath the mucilaginous slime ...

From the novelisation by Pip and Jane Baker (1988)

Unused jacket painting by Alistair Pearson/ Alistrations (1988) for *Doctor Who - The Ultimate Foe.*

Jacket painting by Alistair Pearson/Alistrations (1988) for *Doctor Who - The Ultimate Foe* by Pip and Jane Baker (1988, W. H. Allen & Co. Plc).

convert into a Time Manipulator and recreate the universe. The Doctor manages to stop her. The Doctor and Mel go to a tower block called Paradise Towers for a holiday but find it run down and patrolled by gangs and caretakers. The tower architect's brain is still alive and wants to wipe out everyone living in his creation, but the Doctor manages to escape and the architect is killed. The Doctor helps a

**Above: The Timelords release *Doctorin' the TARDIS* which goes to number one in the record charts (June 1988). Top: To celebrate *Doctor Who*'s twenty fifth anniversary, a first day cover is released (November 1988).**

**The Doctor finds himself faced with a literal cliff-hanger (*Dragonfire* November 1987).**

Chimeron Princess escape the attentions of the Bannermen, led by the evil Gavrok, and then decides to go hunting dragons on the planet Svartos with Sabalom Glitz. Svartos is ruled by Kane, a megalomaniac who wants to return to his own world of Proamon to rule it. The Doctor tells him that Proamon no longer exists and Kane, who can live only in sub-zero conditions, commits suicide by exposing himself to the sun. Mel decides to travel with Sabalom Glitz, and Ace, a young waitress on Svartos, joins the Doctor in the TARDIS.

**[Kane] felt his skin scorching. The searing heat of the sunlight burned into his flesh. His skin began to vapourise in the heat, and steam rose from his body. He opened his mouth wide and screamed in agony.**

**As his flesh melted away, his body began to shrink. He sank to the ground, twisting and screaming with the blinding pain.**

**From the novelisation by Ian Briggs (1989)**

## TV doctor will be the death of me, says Ken

**By GARTH PEARCE**

COMEDIAN Ken Dodd is to play the first death scene in his 30-year career . . . and it is all to save BBC TV's Dr Who from the axe.

The latest Doctor, Sylvester McCoy, and his assistant, played by Bonnie Langford, are being joined by a galaxy of stars to save the ailing show.

Viewing figures have collapsed from 12 million in the show's heyday to about six million.

Ken is to meet his doom at the hands of Don Henderson who plays the detective Bulman in ITV's new series.

### Dramatic

The assignment is worrying Don. " After this I could be known as the man who killed Ken Dodd rather than Bulman," he said yesterday.

But Ken is not too concerned even though the only other dramatic role he has played was as Malvolio in Shakespeare's Twelfth Night.

" My death scene will be one of the longest ever. It's the first one I've ever done and it's my big acting break.

Ken, who plays a galactic gatekeeper in an episode to be screened in November, has joined the cast filming on location in Barry Island, South Wales.

" I can remember watching the very first show," he said. " I've wanted to appear in the series ever since. I just hope it survives."

**Star billing: Bonnie takes time out with Ken**

**Far Left: Press cutting from the *Daily Express* 8 July 1987. Left: A Chimeron (*Delta and the Bannermen* November 1987).**

Jacket painting by Alistair Pearson/Alistrations (1989) for *Doctor Who - Dragonfire* by Ian Briggs (1989, W. H. Allen & Co. Plc).

# Season Twenty Five

The Doctor arrives on Earth in 1963 where the Daleks are planning an attack on Coal Hill School. They are after the Hand of Omega which the Doctor in his first incarnation had secreted on Earth. The Doctor joins forces with the military to defeat both Davros's Imperial Daleks and the renegade Daleks. The TARDIS arrives on the planet Terra Alpha where people must be happy or die. The Doctor helps the inhabitants escape from the rule of Helen

Group Captain Gilmore (Simon Williams), the Doctor and Rachel (Pamela Salem) (*Remembrance of the Daleks* October 1988).

Left: Jon Pertwee and then Colin Baker star as the Doctor in Terrance Dicks' *Doctor Who: The Ultimate Adventure* stage play (March 1989). Right: The Doctor and the Kandyman (David John Pope) (*The Happiness Patrol* November 1988).

## DOCTOR! IT'S THE DALEKS AGAIN

Ex-ter-min-ate! A new Dalek

### By NEIL SYSON

### TV chiefs' ban exterminated

LOOK out, Doctor Who—your enemies the Daleks are back!

BBC telly chiefs have relented after deciding two years ago to exterminate the metal monsters.

They are wheeling on the tinny tyrants to do battle with the Doctor once again in a new series to be screened this autumn.

The Daleks were dropped from the long-running sci-fi show in favour of wacky villains like the intergalactic wideboy Glitz.

And the 25-year-old programme itself looked in danger of the axe when former Beeb chief Michael Grade slated it for being "violent and humourless."

But Mr Grade moved to Channel Four last year and the BBC immediately ordered a new Daleks drama.

Remembrance of the Daleks—starring Sylvester McCoy as the time-travelling Doctor—is being filmed at Hammersmith, West London.

#### Battle

The Daleks are as evil as ever, but they have swapped their dull grey metal jackets for a gold and white livery

Actress Sophie Aldred takes over from Bonnie Langford as the Doctor's new assistant

A BBC spokesman said: "Doctor Who and the Daleks is a tried and tested formula which has succeeded every time.

"The Daleks still have a massive following even though they have not been seen for a few years."

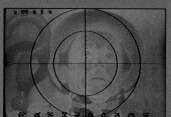

Jacket painting by Alistair
Pearson/Alistrations
(1990) for *Doctor Who -
Remembrance of the
Daleks* by Ben Aaronovitch
(1990, W. H. Allen & Co.
Plc).

A and her robot executioner, the Kandyman. The Doctor returns to present-day Earth to prevent the Cybermen, neo-Nazis and a time-travelling noblewoman called Lady Peinforte from gaining control of the Nemesis statue, made of a Gallifreyan living metal called validium. The statue, which is of Lady Peinforte, hints that the Doctor is not like other Time Lords and that there is more afoot than we realise. The TARDIS picks up an advertising beacon for the Psychic Circus and the Doctor and Ace decide to go to the planet Segonax where it is playing. The circus is actually a trap, designed by the Gods of Ragnarok to provide entertainment and victims for their amusement. The Doctor defeats the Gods and hands the circus over to a band of genuine entertainers, previously slaves to the Gods.

## Magic Moments
*The Greatest Show in the Galaxy* (1988)

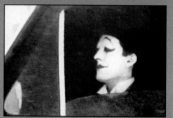

...these undertakers had clowns' faces and the leader, a tall, commanding figure, had a bright red gash of a smile painted across his face at odds not just with his costume but also with the cold blue of the eyes that stood out in the white mask of his make-up. It was a face in which genuine emotion was impossible to read. It was a face both cruel and impassive.

From the novelisation by Stephen Wyatt (1989)

Top: The Cybermen arrive on Earth in search of the Nemesis statue (*Silver Nemesis* November 1988). Far Left Top: The Special Weapons Dalek and its operator Cy Town (*Remembrance of the Daleks* October 1988) GW. Far Left Bottom: A promotional badge for *The Ultimate Adventure*. Left: Writer Terrance Dicks with actors Jon Pertwee, Graeme Smith (Jason) and Rebecca Thornhill (Crystal) at the press launch for *The Ultimate Adventure* (March 1989) DH.

Jacket painting by Alistair Pearson/Alistrations (1993) for Virgin Publishing's re-issue of *Doctor Who - Silver Nemesis* by Kevin Clarke (1989, W. H. Allen & Co. Plc).

# Season Twenty Six

The Doctor receives a distress signal from himself and goes to Earth in the near future to discover that the black witch Morgaine is planning to summon a demon called the Destroyer to annihilate the Earth. The Doctor is recognised as Merlin – one of his future incarnations – and the Brigadier is brought out of retirement to help. He eventually kills the Destroyer with a silver bullet and Morgaine is arrested by UNIT. The Doctor decides to educate Ace, and so takes her back in time to 1883 and an evil house which she burnt down as a young girl in the 1980s. The

Morgaine (Jean Marsh) with Excalibur (*Battlefield* September 1989).

The two Brigadiers: Lethbridge-Stewart (Nicholas Courtney) and Bambara (Angela Bruce) (*Battlefield*).

The Reverend Mr Wainwright (Nicholas Parsons) (*The Curse of Fenric* October 1989) [JML].

Light (John Hallam) awakens (*Ghost Light* October 1989).

## Magic Moments

*The Curse of Fenric (1989)*

After more than a thousand years in the sea, the creatures began to rise. Their abominable forms broke the surface and they started to stride ashore. An army rose from the sea.

Their bodies were horrifying mutations of the humans they had once been. Their skin was slimy and slightly wrinkled, like huge white slugs with legs and arms. Their eyes were swollen and bulbous, closed like a foetus in its uterus. And their mouths had turned into large suckers for draining blood.

From the novelisation by Ian Briggs (1990)

**Left: During studio recording for *Battlefield* Sophie Aldred is involved in a near-fatal accident.**

# DR WHO GIRL CHEATS DEATH

## Sophie is sucked into tank

DR Who's assistant was almost killed and dozens of others had to jump for their lives when a studio stunt went wrong.

The accident happened when actress Sophie Aldred, who plays Ace, was thrown into a glass-lined cylinder full of water.

The glass shattered, sucking Sophie to the bottom of the tank, and sending hundreds of gallons of water flooding on

**By CHARLES CATCHPOLE**

to electrical cables at the BBC Television Centre in West London.

A member of the production team said: "We could all have been killed, as the floor was covered with live cables.

"We jumped on to chairs or hung on to

camera gantries—anything to keep our feet off the ground."

A BBC spokesman said: "Quick thinking prevented a serious disaster.

"Sophie swallowed some water and was shaken, but not hurt."

An inquiry has been launched, but the new series will be ready for the autumn.

SOPHIE: Dice with death

Jacket painting by Alister Pearson/Peter Darvill-Evans (1990) for *Doctor Who - Ghost Light* by Marc Platt (1990, W. H. Allen & Co. Plc).

evil is revealed to be a creature called Light which has been attempting to complete a catalogue of all living things. While Light was dormant its experimental creatures started to evolve and when Light is revived, he decides to destroy the Earth to ensure that his catalogue does not get out of date. The Doctor convinces him that he

too is changing and the creature apparently destroys itself. The Doctor next takes Ace to a secret naval base during the Second World War where his old enemy Fenric is setting up for a final battle. Fenric arranges for the arrival of a race of blood-sucking Hæmovores, and the Doctor saves the day by convincing the Hæmovore leader to

sacrifice itself rather than help Fenric destroy the Earth. Ace wants to return to her home in Perivale and the Doctor takes her there, only to become involved in the Master's plot to escape from the doomed planet of the Cheetah People. The Doctor escapes with his life and he and Ace leave for further adventures in time and space.

The Doctor and Ace (Sophie Aldred) (*The Curse of Fenric* October 1989).

The Cheetah people on their doomed planet (*Survival* November 1989).

Ace and the neanderthal butler Nimrod (Carl Forgione) (*Ghost Light* October 1989).

'Let's go back to the TARDIS,' the Doctor said gently.
Ace looked up at him.
He smiled at her. 'Let's go home, Ace.'
Arm in arm they walked away.

From the novelisation by Rona Munro (1990)

## NEW FUTURE FOR Dr WHO

DR WHO could soon be leaving the BBC. But fans of the Time Lord need not worry.

Plans are afoot to farm it out to an independent production company. The series will be rested next year — and blast back better than ever.

Our Beeb mole said: "The BBC believe it will be bigger and better in an independent's hands. And all the stars will remain the same."

Watch out for the Doctor — Sylvester McCoy — in a new series starting tonight.

Above: Press cutting from the *Sport* 6 October 1989. Right: The Destroyer (Marek Anton), summoned by Morgaine to destroy the Earth (*Battlefield* September 1989) SM.

Ace in the Churchyard of St Jude's (*The Curse of Fenric*) JML.

Jacket painting by Alistair Pearson/Allstrations (1990) for *Doctor Who - Survival* by Rona Munro (1990, W. H. Allen & Co. Plc).

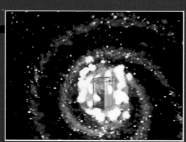

# THE NINETIES

**T**he last newly made *Doctor Who* stories were transmitted on BBC television in 1989. Though the BBC was apparently uninterested in continuing the series, other companies were. The BBC, however, refused to sell the rights, to make further episodes themselves or to explain exactly what their plans for the series were. Despite this, interest in the programme continued unabated. Both Virgin Publishing (originally W. H. Allen) and Marvel Comics continued the Doctor's adventures with an interconnected series of books and comic strips written both by fans and by people who had been connected with the TV series. *Doctor Who* in both these forms was phenomenally successful, as were the videos of past adventures which BBC Enterprises started to release on a more regular basis. *Doctor Who* also moved on to audio cassette as the BBC released some adventures missing from the film and television archives but still existing on audiotape. There was more interest from merchandisers, with new Dalek toys, books, a chess set, tankards, crockery and even a

pinball machine being released. *Doctor Who* was again re-peated on BBC television, and satellite channels showed many old stories. The BBC sold off many original *Doctor Who* cos-tumes and props, and these well-attended auctions raised many tens of thousands of pounds for the corporation. A huge *Doctor Who* exhibition was staged at London's Museum of the Moving Image, and staff there reported a significant up-swing in attendance and interest during its run. Such was the exhibition's popularity that it was extended from its initial run of three months, to one of just under a year. In 1993, to celebrate thirty years of *Doctor Who*, a massive convention was organised in London, the BBC commissioned a new docu-mentary on the series, and six specially made five minute mini-documentaries were recorded to accompany a repeat showing of *Planet of the Daleks* on BBC1. There was a char-ity two-part *Doctor Who* skit *Dimensions in Time* made for the *Children In Need* appeal which featured all the Doctors and most of the companions and, towards the end of 1993, Steven Spielberg was rumoured to be in serious discussion with the BBC about the future of the series.

After thirty years, the magic of *Doctor Who* was still going strong . . .

# The New Adventures

## TIMEWYRM:
## Genesys
## Exodus
## Apocalypse
## Revelation

The TARDIS arrives in Mesopotamia where an alien called Ishtar is trying to conquer the Earth. The creature invades the TARDIS and, due to a miscalculation on the Doctor's part, gains the power of time travel and becomes the Timewyrm. The Doctor and Ace must track it down and prevent it from altering history. They trace it to London in 1951, but time has been altered: with the help of the Timewyrm, Hitler won the Second World War and Britain is now a part of the German Reich. The Doctor manages to undo the Timewyrm's meddling and discovers that the renegade Time Lord War Chief and his Alien allies were also involved, having been attracted by Hitler's apparent telepathic powers. The Doctor next tracks the Timewyrm to the planet Kirith where he helps a civilisation regain its feet. Finally, the Timewyrm invades the Doctor's mind, turning Ace against him. In a literal battle of wills, the Doctor defeats the Timewyrm.

A promotional poster for *Doctor Who: Last of the Time Lords* is produced for the MIFED Film Festival in October 1990. By 1993 there is still no sign of production starting on the film.

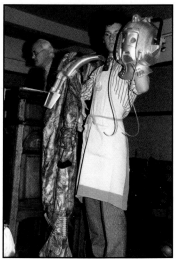

Top: Marvel Comics release the first of their *Doctor Who* yearbooks (July 1991). Above: Numerous *Doctor Who* costumes are auctioned off by the BBC in four well attended sales (August 1990, May 1991, August 1991, August 1992). The Cyberman costume pictured above is a reproduction which went for £1300 at the third sale [DH]. Below: Elisabeth Sladen talks about *Doctor Who* at a lecture held at London's MOMI exhibition (November 1991). [DH]

Left, and Above: The satellite channel BSB devotes a whole weekend to *Doctor Who* repeats, interviews and special presentations. The weekend is hosted by John Nathan-Turner, Debbie Flint and Shyama Perera (22-23 September 1990) [DH].

The first title in *The New Adventures* range is published (20 June 1991): *The New Doctor Who Adventures - Timewyrm: Genesys.*

Jacket painting by Andrew Skilleter (1991) for *Doctor Who The New Adventures: Timewyrm - Apocalypse* by Nigel Robinson (1991, Virgin Publishing Ltd).

## CAT'S CRADLE:
## Time's Crucible
## Warhead
## Witch Mark

**D**amaged in its battle with the Timewyrm, the TARDIS turns itself inside out. The Doctor and Ace find themselves up against the Process, a leech-like monster, in a nightmare, time-distorted world inside the time machine. On Earth in the future, the Doctor and Ace work to prevent an industrialist from taking the ultimate step to convert human beings into computers. They succeed but when they try to have a rest, they become caught up in the plans of the inhabitants of Tir na n-Og to use Earth as an escape route from their own world, which is under attack by Goibhnie – an alien conducting experiments in evolution.

### Summoned by Shadows
by Christian Darkin

After many wanderings through time and space, the mysterious traveller (**Colin Baker**) now ekes out an existence in solitude and self-obsession...

**Summoned by Shadows**

**Summoned by Shadows**

# Summoned by Shadows

by Christian Darkin

Starring
**COLIN BAKER and NICOLA BRYANT**

"The best in surreal, comp... discerning SF
*Gareth Pickard, magazine*

"A mesmerising, morbidly fascinating tale, empowered by outstanding performances, this Kafka-esque psychodrama, packs punch with insight, a unique and terrifying experience..."
*F.F., Science Fiction and Fantasy Review.*

Directed and Produced by Bill Baggs
Running time: 40 min approx

**BBV 1**

The BBC Film Club produces the first in a series of video dramas featuring a mysterious Stranger (Colin Baker) and his assistant Miss Brown (Nicola Bryant). *Summoned By Shadows* (1991) is the first release and it is followed by *More than a Messiah* (1992) which guest-stars Sophie Aldred (inset photograph) [RP].

A large *Doctor Who* exhibition opens at the Museum of the Moving Image in London. At its launch, several *Doctor Who* 'girls' are present to cut the Dalek-shaped cake which has been made especially for the event by Jane Asher (July 1991) [DH].

BEHIND THE SOFA
THE DOCTOR WHO EXHIBITION AT MOMI

BEHIND THE SOFA
THE DOCTOR WHO EXHIBITION AT MOMI

Doctor Who at MOMI

Jacket painting by Peter Elson/Sarah Brown Artists Agency (1992) for *Doctor Who The New Adventures: Cat's Cradle - Witch Mark* by Andrew Hunt (1992, Virgin Publishing Ltd).

## Nightshade
## Love and War
## Transit
## The Highest Science
## The Pit
## Deceit
## Lucifer Rising

**O**n Earth in 1968, an unearthly force is resurrecting phantoms from the past to haunt the inhabitants of the village of Crook Marsham. The Doctor realises the seriousness of the threat and with the help of an elderly actor, Edmund Trevithick, manages to confront and send the malignant force out into space. Deciding to explore the future history of Earth and its colonies, the Doctor and Ace arrive on the planet Heaven only to find themselves caught up in an invasion by the alien Hoothi. Ace, disgusted with the Doctor's callous use of others, stays behind on Heaven while the Doctor travels on with a young archæologist called Bernice Summerfield. Their first journey takes them to the near future where an interplanetary transit system has been invaded by a computer virus which the Doctor isolates and defeats. A phenomenon called a Fortean Flicker has brought several disparate groups to the lost planet of Sakkrat: a war force of Chelonians, a group of youngsters en route to a pop concert and a carriage from the eight twelve train from Amersham to Aldgate. The Doctor investigates the source of the Flicker and discovers that the planet is not what it seems. Bernice then suggests they investigate the Seven Planets, which mysteriously disappeared years before she was born. When they arrive on one of them, they find killer

androids hunting two shape-changing criminals and a terrible enemy from Gallifrey's past. Their next trip reunites them with Ace, but three years of fighting Daleks in Spacefleet's Irregular Auxiliaries have changed her. After confronting a horribly powerful being on the paradise planet of Arcadia, Ace rejoins the TARDIS crew and persuades them to travel to Lucifer pursuing her own agenda. They become involved in sabotage, murder and the resurrection of eons-old alien powers.

**MBI start taking subscriptions for an impressive but expensive *Doctor Who* chess set (1992).**

**Above and Below: *Doctor Who* arrives on computer as Alternative Software release their *Dalek Attack* game (November 1992).**

**Reeltime Pictures follow up the huge success of their initial Tom Baker interview tape with a second video, this time featuring Baker talking to Baker about Baker (August 1991).**

***Return to Devil's End* is another Reeltime Pictures project, this time re-uniting some of the cast and crew of the third Doctor adventure *The Daemons* at the village in which the original story was made (January 1993).**

**A copy of the 'lost' second Doctor adventure *The Tomb of the Cybermen* is returned from Hong Kong in January 1992 and is quickly released on video. In ten days it sells 25,000 units and tops the video charts for the period (May 1992).**

Jacket painting by Luis Rey/Sarah Brown Artists Agency (1993) for *Doctor Who The New Adventures: Deceit* by Peter Darvill-Evans (1993, Virgin Publishing Ltd).

## White Darkness
## Shadowmind
## Birthright
## Iceberg

The TARDIS crew go to Haiti in 1915 and find revolution brewing in the city, the dead walking and a secret German base hidden beneath the mountains. Wanting a holiday, the Doctor takes Ace and Bernice to peaceful Tairngire. However something there is very wrong: people who leave the planet are coming back changed. Realising that if they can't take a holiday together, they must take one apart, the Doctor leaves Ace and Bernice to face an Edwardian sorcerer and an alien insect-like race, while he travels to Antarctica in the near future, where he finds the Cybermen hidden beneath the ice.

## Blood Heat
## The Dimension Riders
## The Left-Handed Hummingbird

The Doctor realises that someone or something is tampering with his past, when he discovers that Earth is now ruled by reptiles. Setting history back on course, the Doctor finds himself battling a powerful enemy in deep space, and then pitting his wits against an ancient Aztec god who should never have existed.

Something or someone seems determined to alter history, but can the Doctor prevent it?

Thus the epic voyage of the Doctor reaches the end of its thirtieth year with the Doctor locked in battle against an unknown and powerful adversary. The future holds more adventures and more surprises, but this chronicle ends here.

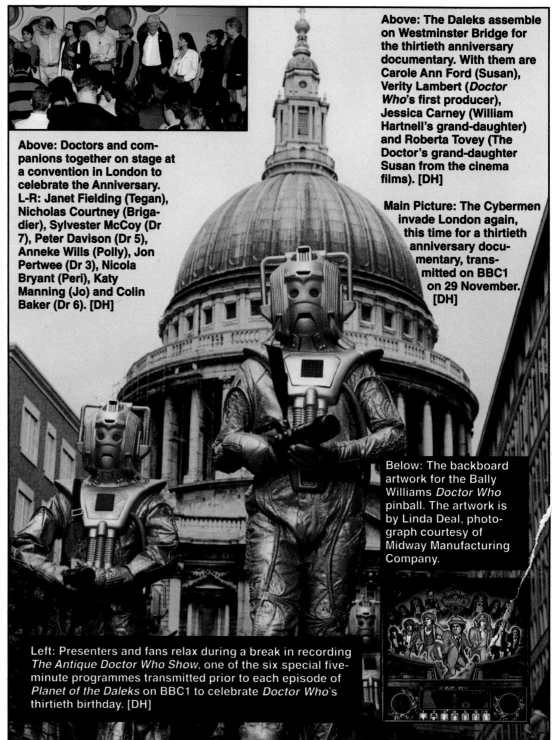

Above: Doctors and companions together on stage at a convention in London to celebrate the Anniversary. L-R: Janet Fielding (Tegan), Nicholas Courtney (Brigadier), Sylvester McCoy (Dr 7), Peter Davison (Dr 5), Anneke Wills (Polly), Jon Pertwee (Dr 3), Nicola Bryant (Peri), Katy Manning (Jo) and Colin Baker (Dr 6). [DH]

Above: The Daleks assemble on Westminster Bridge for the thirtieth anniversary documentary. With them are Carole Ann Ford (Susan), Verity Lambert (*Doctor Who*'s first producer), Jessica Carney (William Hartnell's grand-daughter) and Roberta Tovey (The Doctor's grand-daughter Susan from the cinema films). [DH]

Main Picture: The Cybermen invade London again, this time for a thirtieth anniversary documentary, transmitted on BBC1 on 29 November. [DH]

Below: The backboard artwork for the Bally Williams *Doctor Who* pinball. The artwork is by Linda Deal, photograph courtesy of Midway Manufacturing Company.

Left: Presenters and fans relax during a break in recording *The Antique Doctor Who Show*, one of the six special five-minute programmes transmitted prior to each episode of *Planet of the Daleks* on BBC1 to celebrate *Doctor Who*'s thirtieth birthday. [DH]

**Jacket painting by Peter Elson/Sarah Brown Artists Agency (1993) for *Doctor Who The New Adventures: Birthright* by Nigel Robinson (1993, Virgin Publishing Ltd).**

Two pieces of artwork completed by Jeff Cummins in the late seventies for a projected *Doctor Who* calendar which was never produced.
Top: *The Pyramids of Mars*.
Bottom: *The Sea Devils*.